Caring That Enables

A Manual for Developing Parish Family Ministry

Leif Kehrwald

PAULIST PRESS

NEW YORK / MAHWAH

Library of Congress Cataloging-in-Publication Data

Kehrwald, Leif, 1957–
     Caring that enables : a manual for developing parish family
ministry / Leif Kehrwald.
          p.   cm.
     ISBN 0-8091-3240-0
     1. Church work with families—Catholic Church.   I. Title.
BX2347.8.F3K34   1991
259'.1—dc20   91-12721
                                                        CIP

Published by Paulist Press
997 Macarthur Boulevard
Mahwah, NJ 07430

Printed and bound in the
United States of America

Contents

I   Families, Parishes and Family Ministry   1

II   Implementing the Project   15

III   Training Session #1   22
Family Life Awareness Raising

IV   Training Session #2   35
Bringing a Family Sensitivity to Parish Ministry

V   Training Session #3   52
Focus and Invite

VI   Training Session #4   79
*Assessment of Team Progress and
Developing Leadership in Parish Family Ministry*

VII   Conclusion   91

Acknowledgments

This manual became possible because of the support of many people. My appreciation and gratitude go to all of them. To the folks I worked with in Spokane, Washington, particularly Mary Bressler, Sr. Donna Storms, F.S.P.A., Rev. Michael Savelesky and Betty Mathers, who encouraged and supported me in developing the strategies for *Caring That Enables*. To those I work with in Portland, Oregon, Kathleen Truman and Rev. Richard Huneger, who now provide similar support. To all the pastors and parish leaders who have worked with these strategies, made them come alive and provided extremely valuable feedback and insights. To my colleagues in family ministry around the country, particularly Cathy Billings, who have encouraged me to write down my ideas for parish family ministry. To Georgia Christo and Paulist Press who showed interest in and enthusiasm for my work and the courage to publish it. To Rev. Tom Lynch who provided the spark for the ideas of this manual. To Kathy Schaeffer and David Thomas of the Masters in Christian Community Development Program at Regis College, Denver, who provided an atmosphere for me to learn about writing, and encouraged me to write this manual. I greatly appreciate my own parents, Dick and Carrie Kehrwald, who provided me with a healthy and loving family life. Above all, I am grateful to Rene, my wife, whose patience and encouragement never ceased throughout this entire project. Because of these special persons, I was empowered to write this manual.

I Families, Parishes and Family Ministry

What's a Family Anyway?

I once met with a group of parish volunteers to discuss issues and struggles facing today's American families. Most of the issues you would mention surfaced: divorce, single-parenthood, dual employed households, family priorities, scary consequences for experimental behavior, peer pressure, materialism, poverty, abuse, blended families, high mobility, lack of bondedness, etc., etc.

Before long, we concluded there is no such thing as a typical American family. The "traditional" nuclear family of a working father, stay-at-home mother with several children comprises a very low percentage of American households. Our society today contains many different forms of family life.

So then someone asked, "What do you mean by 'family' anyway?" I felt obligated to supply an answer—but I was stumped. I knew that a purely sociological definition such as "a group of persons related by blood, marriage or adoption" would sound too dry and clinical with this group. I also knew that an idealistic definition such as "a community of persons bonded together for love and nurturing" would be too glib and elevated.

What's the right definition of family? We concluded that for the purposes of our discussions we could use the words "family" and "household" interchangeably. We all agreed that they are not exactly the same thing, but the lived reality of most folks allows us to draw many connections between their household life and their family life.

That group was a volunteer parish family ministry team gathered for their first training session of the *Caring That Enables* project.

1

The same conclusions will hold true for this manual. We may be evading the question of definition of family, but for our purposes we can use "family" and "household" interchangeably.

How do we gain a better understanding of family/household life? A brief historical perspective will help. My friend and colleague Dennis Keenan has shared with me an interesting way to look at the recent evolution of family life in America. He likens family members and their functions to threads in fabric. I first wrote about the "family fabric" in the June 1988 issue of *Catholic Update*, "Making Family a Priority in Your Parish." Below is an excerpt from that article.

The Family Fabric

The fabric of American family life has changed dramatically over the last one hundred and fifty years. In the *agricultural* era, most families earned their living from the land. As a result, family units were necessarily large, often comprised of grandparents, aunts and uncles, as well as many children. Each member contributed to the livelihood of the household.

Consequently, the important functions of education, vocational choice, health care, religious formation, recreation, personal nurturing and reproduction were accomplished primarily by the family. Even choosing a spouse was a family matter which affected land acquisition and economics. The family fabric was tightly woven with many threads during that era. If a marriage was on the rocks, or a child had a problem, these broken threads were held in place by the rest of the fabric.

The *industrial revolution* exerted a major impact on this family fabric. The threads of economics, education and health care were pulled from the family and handed to institutions of society. Family size began to shrink as families moved to industrial centers. The family held onto the key threads of personal nurturing and reproduction, and entered into partnerships with several institutions (church, recreation leagues, etc.) over the remaining threads. The family fabric remained secure, yet clearly fewer threads were holding the family in place.

In today's *technological society*, families are highly mobile with fewer members. The average household is comprised of just under three persons. Nearly all major family functions have been usurped by a host of service organizations. The only two threads families have retained since the agricultural era are personal nurturing and reproduction. Even the nurturing function is shared with child-care agencies by many two-carner and single-parent families.

The fabric of today's family is thin and vulnerable. When a marriage is in a crisis, or a child exhibits disruptive behavior, the fabric cannot hold those broken threads in place. Life is completely disrupted for all, often causing a chain reaction of more struggles and problems.

Families have lost their share of control over many important functions. A return to the agricultural era is not possible, so families must seek a renewed partnership with the organizations designed to serve their needs. The parish is certainly one such organization. This renewed partnership does not necessarily mean new parish programs for families, but rather adjusting programs with a family sensitivity.

Responding to Today's Family Fabric

Most people are generally aware of the thin family fabric of today. Yet many, in the context of their church, hold on emotionally to the notion that family really means the "traditional," intact, nuclear household. The portrait of American family life is much different from what we were raised to believe it should be. Because of the rapid changes in our society, families are struggling to keep up, and many stumble along the way. Most folks will readily agree that divorce and remarriage play a large and significant role in our communities. They recognize the high percentage of women with children who are employed outside the home, and the growing industry of child care. Yet, for some people, the word "family" still enjoys a rather narrow meaning.

The first strategy of this manual is called Family Life Awareness Raising (Chapter III). It is an attempt to broaden the meaning and reality of family life for all parishioners. It attempts to bridge the clutter and chaos of household life with the neat and tidy structure of parish life.

Through this strategy parishioners will be exposed to facts and statistics about family living as they pertain to such issues as divorce, single-parenting, two earner families, child care, family size and mobility, aging, family crises, etc. They will also be given tips and ideas on healthy family living focused on areas such as parenting, communication, developing family priorities, etc. And they may even be introduced to quotations concerning family life. One of my favorites came from Paul Tsongas when he retired from the U.S. Senate: "I've yet to meet anyone who chose family over career and regretted it. No one on his deathbed ever said, 'I didn't spend enough time with my business.'"

The second strategy presented in this manual (Chapter IV) provides the volunteer family ministry team with a myriad of first-step ideas for bringing a family sensitivity to parish ministries and services.

Some would say that in light of the realities of today's families, and their crucial needs, parishes should close down all programs and rebuild everything with a family focus. It would be nice if all parishes did that, but it is just not realistic. Therefore, a family perspective in the parish requires a slow and steady shift of posture of *existing programs* toward a renewed partnership with household life.

Sometimes we compete with households for their time, energy and space as we sponsor our programs and services. We become frustrated when folks don't show up after we've spent so much of our own time and energy planning the program. We conclude that they just don't care and that their priorities are misaligned. This may be true for some families, but others may simply be placing a priority on being home. We may have been competing for their last small portion of family prime time.

We need to move to a more cooperative approach that respects the rhythms and dynamics of today's hectic household living. Most parish ministries and programs can find simple ways to adjust their services (scheduling, providing child care, etc.) to adopt a more cooperative approach. Numerous practical ideas are mentioned in Chapter IV, all of which have been implemented by volunteer folks in the parish.

The thin family fabric as described above also indicates the great need for like-to-like support and resourcing for families of all forms and at all stages. Chapter V attempts to address this need. In a simple, do-able, first-step fashion the volunteer family ministry team will invite folks of similar needs and concerns to gather for mutual sharing, support and ongoing enrichment.

When the nuclear household has shrunk to just three or four persons, whether intact or not, they need help and support from others just to negotiate the challenging tasks presented at each stage of family maturity. In other words, our parish and community neighbors must fulfill the role that the extended family played in generations past.

For example, your family may be experiencing the confusion and chaos of early adolescence, and feeling very alone. Parent anxiety rises as the stakes for experimental behavior rise. The higher your anxiety, the harder it is to be a good parent. You can't think straight, and your confidence is low. Young teens pick that up very quickly, and, in their own way, take advantage.

Parents often worry if their child's behavior is "disturbed" or just "disturbing." If it is just disturbing, then the parent must draw upon his/her best skills and attitudes to maintain harmony and sanity in the household. If it is disturbed behavior, he/she needs to seek help. Trying to determine the difference while isolated from other parents is extremely difficult.

But if parents have a chance to talk about similar concerns and needs, they can put their anxiety into perspective, and view their situations more clearly. Chances are it is just "disturbing" behavior, and simply commiserating with others will make one feel better. With luck, a parent may come away with a new parenting tip or strategy to try out. If, after sharing with others, a parent thinks it might be "disturbed" behavior, then he/she can garner the emotional support needed to seek help.

Family Life and the Parish

I know a family who recently moved to a new city. They chose where to live based on the parish community they wanted to join. Meaningful worship and quality Christian education were key factors for their choice of residence.

This family has always maintained an intimate relationship with their parish. Although many families are not as deliberate in that relationship, I believe there is a strong, inherent link between families and their worshiping community.

The documents of Vatican II referred to the Christian family as the "domestic church." Under the premise of "where two or three are gathered in my name, I am in their midst," Christian families can choose to be church. David Thomas, a noted family theologian, refers to the family as "foundational church." Yet many couples, parents and families do not realize that God is fully present and active in their households. They have to go to their church to find God. For generations it has been implied that the parish is the focal point of one's faith activity. From God's point of view, however, our distinctions between church and home, sacred and secular, are irrelevant. God can only be fully present.

Yet families cannot be church in isolation. They need their parish. The basis of Christian living is community. No one person or household has an exclusive on the "truth." When we align ourselves together along common beliefs, our vision and experience of God is much more keen. And so, families need the parish community in order to maintain themselves as a healthy domestic church. The parish community can also contribute to many of the family's social and educational needs.

Likewise, the parish needs healthy families. The quality of community, worship, Christian education and apostolic service expressed by the parish is directly related to the quality of household life. The expression of Christian values shared in the home, and passed on from one generation to the next, builds a foundation for the same expression in the larger community of the parish.

Therefore, it is in the best interest of the parish to support and nurture family living. We cannot force families to explore the presence of God in their midst, but we can create a better atmosphere for them to do so.

I once met with a group of parish leaders representing all facets of ministry in their parish. The focus of the meeting was family life: how to meet the needs of families and enrich household life. I conducted a group exercise that proved to be revelatory for all of us. First, I asked them to mention all the ministries and services available in the parish. I wrote them on the board: Knights of Columbus, Altar Society, Religious Education, Youth Group, Parish Council, Bible Study Group, Choir, etc. They were a typical parish with the typical groups and services.

Moving to the other side of the board, I asked them to brainstorm the issues, concerns, and struggles that families and households of the parish find themselves dealing with: divorce, unemployment, blended families, adequate housing, parent-teen relationships, financial burdens, parenting struggles, etc. Again, they mentioned many of the typical family issues of our day.

With the two lists side by side, they quickly realized that of all the activities in their parish, few directly attempted to strengthen family living. Someone said the parish needed new programs. But then someone else suggested that perhaps several existing programs could make some adjustments to begin filling in the void. Much to my delight, the group agreed with the second person, and we spent the remainder of our time discussing ways of bringing a family perspective to existing parish ministries. This isn't to say that developing new programs for families doesn't have value. My point was that since the parish already had so many things going on, it would be difficult to initiate new programs *without further fragmenting household life in the process*. Besides, whom could they get to coordinate and maintain new programs?

If the parish can shift its posture toward a better understanding of the day-to-day realities of household living, families will be more likely to put a greater stake in their parish. Normally this shift begins with secular, human matters such as child care, relationship building, parenting, family finances, etc. If the parish can be genuinely present to them here, then, in God's time, families will take a greater interest in faith expression.

How can the parish shift its posture? Addressing this question is one of the primary goals of this manual. In addition to the specific strategies presented, I have three general reminders for parish leaders.

Reminder #1. All parish programs and services impact family life. Some have positive impact; others negative. As parish leaders, we tend to focus our ministry efforts in two areas: the individual and the community. This is by no means wrong. Sometimes, though, family life is fragmented in the process.

It is appropriate, for example, that the parish RCIA process focus on individuals—the catechumens. Yet if the process does not take into account the household members of each catechumen, then those families will resist the change required in accepting someone's faith growth. Hence the process of conversion may be incomplete.

As another example, a parish renewal program justifiably places a strong emphasis on community building. Yet the efforts employed should not hinder household living by calling folks away from their families for numerous meetings, etc. Parish renewal should be linked to household renewal.

When parish leaders recognize that all services and programs impact family life, they can work toward a harmonious rather than competitive relationship with families.

Reminder #2. Change is most effective one small step at a time. Persons and communities naturally resist change. According to the revelations of systems theory, genuine change is resisted because it upsets the working balance of the system. Whether the system is a family or a parish, it operates with a certain set of "rules" and "roles." Each member consciously or unconsciously knows his or her part, and the general rules of interaction. When a member of the system acts differently or does not abide by the "rules," the other members will naturally resist, *even if the change is a positive one.*

Bringing a family perspective to parish ministry involves changing attitudes, convictions and actions. This does not happen overnight. Yet if the parish family ministry team can steadily influence a variety of ministries and parish leaders, then in time the posture of the entire parish will shift. As this happens, people's attitudes and expectations will begin to reflect a stronger sensitivity to family issues. When people's convictions change, their actions follow suit.

I once heard someone suggest that if a parish was serious about being a family oriented community, it should shut down all programs and services and rebuild from scratch with family life as a focal point. Even if this were feasible I am not convinced this action would yield the desired result. Why? Too many parishioners are emotionally or nostalgically tied to one structure or another. Take those structures away, and we lose the support and allegiance of these parishioners to the community.

Yet, if we introduce simple adjustments that bring a family perspective to these programs, people maintain their investment. Parish leaders and parishioners are not intentionally anti-family. But many will not support family ministry if their "pet service" appears threatened.

Reminder #3. Challenge—gently, of course—pastors and key parish leaders to view their ministry through a family lens. It is a myth that effective ministry to individuals automatically implies effective ministry to the families of those individuals. It is also a myth that creative parish community building automatically benefits families in the community. This may prove true in some parishes, but it is not automatic.

However, it is a fact that incorporating a family perspective in any service or ministry will not only enrich family living, but will also enhance the quality of that particular ministry. When pastors and parish leaders realize that this effort does not require a complete overhaul of existing programs or even starting new ones, they will be more open to making the simple adjustments that may be needed. When we can demonstrate how a family perspective will benefit their particular ministry, then we've got them on our side, and they will work hard to make the adjustments.

The three strategies presented in this manual are good for parish life as well as family life. The first strategy, *family life awareness raising*, will bridge the clutter and chaos of everyday household life with the spiritual endeavors of the parish community. The church has always voiced high ideals for family life, but, as a family person, I sometimes wonder if my parish really understands the normal "craziness" of my home.

The second strategy, *family sensitivity in parish ministry*, enriches parish life by challenging parish leaders to filter their efforts through a family lens. More (activities, programs, services) is not always better. A healthy parish works within the rhythms of household life, not in a posture of competing with them for time, space and energy.

The third strategy, *focus and invite*, nearly always serves as a terrific parish community builder. Granted, not all parishioners are invited to the gathering. Yet when some folks experience support and nurturing from others of similar needs and concerns, it is reflected in the quality of Sunday worship as well as other aspects of parish life.

A clearer description of these strategies concludes this chapter, but first let me offer a reflection on family spirituality.

A Word About Family Spirituality

If Jesus was born into your household last Christmas, and then lived with you and your family for thirty years, would he still succeed with his ministry, death and resurrection? Think about it.

The answer: absolutely *yes*!

He would succeed not just because Jesus is God, and God can

overcome any obstacle (even your household), but because your house is *holy*. This is family spirituality in a nutshell. Your house is holy. Amid the chaos and clutter of everyday living, amid the confusion and brokenness of strained relationships, or perhaps amid the lonesomeness of a single person dwelling, God is present and active.

Jesus spent thirty years preparing for our salvation living in an ordinary family in an ordinary community. His parents were faithful to Yahweh and participated in the community of believers. Jesus' formation as a child was not unique. But because he did succeed with his ministry, death and resurrection, he legitimized the holy and sacred nature of family living.

God is present and active in *all* households, not just those who do religious activities at home. God does not discriminate between "churchy" activities and those of regular secular life. He can't! As creator of all things, God sees all as holy and sacred. God is just as present at the Sunday breakfast table and even the Saturday evening argument over curfew as at Sunday mass. God can only be *fully present*.

In developing family spirituality, we err when we only give folks ideas for "churchy" activities to do at home. We must also help them create an atmosphere in the home where they can discover God's genuine presence. It might well happen as they share Bible stories at the dinner table or sing around the Advent wreath. Many Christian families are deliberate in their choice to express their faith and values in the home, and are looking for creative resources that assist them.

Yet many other folks are not in a posture of making those deliberate choices, but God is still present and active in their lives. This activity, I believe, is discoverable in the regular stuff of life: a discussion about a movie, or commiserating over grandma's death. In the right atmosphere, God's grace can explode.

The strategies for family ministry presented in this manual can cultivate family spirituality. Even though they are designed to enrich family health in general, family spirituality is a key health factor. Therefore, Chapters III through V which describe each family ministry strategy in detail each contain a section on family spirituality. It is an important concept which must be integrated into all our efforts.

The Challenge of Family Ministry

Given everything said thus far, the question we seek to answer is simply: How do we do family ministry? How do we begin to enrich household life and meet some of the educational, formational and spiritual needs of families? The strategies presented in this manual are first step ideas for doing just that. They have been tested and used in over twenty-five parishes and have been adapted in many creative ways. And they work.

Parishes must be challenged to resource families to meet their ever changing social, pastoral and educational needs. This manual is a useful tool to help parish leaders do this.

The *Caring That Enables* manual is focused around three specific challenges for family ministry:

- *To implement at the parish level.* The future of family ministry lies in the parish, not in the diocesan Family Life Office. One must recognize the intimate relationship between family life and parish life.
- *To implement with volunteer leadership.* The last thing parish pastoral leaders need is another area of ministry to add to their job description. Pastors, associates, directors of religious education and other parish staff members sincerely recognize the need for healthy family life. However, most do not have time or energy to add more programs to their bulging schedules. Therefore, the ministry to families must rely on volunteer leadership—recognizing their own limitations of time, energy and expertise.
- *To implement without creating new parish programs.* Today's families are extremely busy, and parish calendars are so full that sponsoring more meetings at the parish can actually fragment family life and over-burden parish leaders. What can be done without creating new parish programs?

Given these challenges, I developed the three strategies for family ministry. I then tested and refined them with nearly twenty-five parish volunteer teams in the diocese of Spokane, Washington and the archdiocese of Portland, Oregon. The three strategies—*family life awareness raising, family sensitivity in parish ministry,* and *focus and invite*—are not the only possibilities for parish family ministry, but they can be implemented at the parish level, with volunteer leadership, and without creating new parish programs.

Three Simple Strategies

• *Family Life Awareness Raising.*
This strategy heightens parishioner awareness of the realities of family life today. We all know there are many varieties of families in our society—blended, divorced, dual earner, single-parent, mixed race, etc. Yet many parishioners hold on to the old traditional myth that "family" really means an intact marriage and household. Not so. Each family form must be accepted and embraced by the parish, and then challenged to share its healthy family traits.

Through the various forms of parish communication, *family life awareness raising* challenges parishioners to embrace all the different expressions of family life in the parish and in society. This is done through the Sunday bulletin, prayers of the faithful, notes home through children, preaching from the pulpit, etc.

The idea is to provoke thought about family related issues, concerns and realities. You won't be asking anyone to do anything or come to anything. It is simply a piece of interesting information, and it's free. Chapter III covers all the specifics about implementing the strategy of family life awareness raising.

• *Family Sensitivity in Parish Ministry.*

> No plan of organized pastoral work at any level must ever
> fail to take into consideration the pastoral area of the family.
> *Familiaris Consortio #70*

This strategy calls for a partnership between the volunteer family ministry team and leaders of other services in the parish. Their task together is to evaluate the particular service from the viewpoint of household life. What impact does this ministry have on families — positive or negative? What adjustments can be made to be more sensitive to today's families?

Many parish ministries are structured around either one or two specific focal points: the individual and/or the parish community. Neither emphasis is bad, unless families are fragmented in the process. A family perspective challenges parish leaders to evaluate their efforts through a family lens and make necessary adjustments.

The variety of simple adjustments which can be made to incorporate a family perspective is endless. Chapter IV gives step by step instructions for how the family ministry team can partner with other parish ministries. This chapter also contains numerous, practical examples for bringing a family sensitivity to parish ministry.

• *Focus and Invite.*
This strategy brings parents and/or families of like-needs and like-concerns together for mutual support and encouragement.

The team first learns the key principles of family life cycle theory. This theory recognizes that most families experience similar changes and struggles at relatively predictable periods throughout the family's development.

Next, the team analyzes parish census information to decide which group of parents or families to *focus* on. They may choose parents of adolescents, or single-parent households, or pre-school families, etc. It is important for the team to learn as much as they can about this group and gather pertinent resources (books, articles, lists of referral services, even video programs) to make available to them.

Through a personal letter and follow-up phone call, members of the focus group are then *invited* to meet for one session. They will discuss their common issues and concerns, draw support from one another, investigate available resources, and explore options for ongoing support and education.

The focus and invite gatherings, above all, allow participants to see that they are not alone in their family struggles, concerns and joys. Ample time for sharing must be structured into the session.

Many teams choose to have a guest speaker for part of the evening. Others simply ask a parent or couple who have "lived through" that stage of family life to share a few tips, anecdotes and reflections.

During the last part of the evening, the family ministry team presents several options for ongoing support and education. The key to these options is that they be simple, short-term and easy to implement. Chapter V outlines the focus and invite strategy in detail.

The Strategies Work

Implementing these strategies will not only enrich family life, they will also enhance parish life. Parishes who have worked with these strategies have found, over time, that the partnership between households and the parish community is warmer and stronger. By that I mean that there is a greater degree of honesty and endearment between the two. For some families, the parish takes on a more prominent role in their lives. For some parishioners, family life takes on a new and different perspective, whether in their own home or in their service to others. In either case, the link between parish and household is strengthened, and both benefit.

II Implementing the Project

This chapter tells how to implement *Caring That Enables*. As with any project, pre-planning and organization are important keys to success. I am the type of person who plans well in advance and outlines a project step-by-step. You will find that this manual follows suit.

Yet I am aware that writing out the strategies with clear, step-by-step instructions can make the project appear highly structured and unimaginative. *You* have to bring life and creativity to it. Feel free to proceed with an idea of your own, or improve on the suggestions I make. Each parish team I have instructed has adapted the three strategies of *Caring That Enables* to suit their parish situation. I take that as a compliment. I am glad to have stimulated others' imagination and creativity.

So that you may benefit from this creativity, I have included several variations of each strategy that other parishes have used. These ideas will assist your planning and organization.

Getting Started: Read through the *Caring That Enables* Manual

The fact that you have this manual in hand, and have read this far, indicates that you are serious about doing family ministry in your parish. This chapter gives all the directions you need to begin, but be sure to read the entire manual before executing the first steps. Doing so will give you the overall picture of the training sessions and how to facilitate the entire project. You might also think of adaptations that will benefit your particular parish situation.

The Project Coordinator

Parish teams who have done well with *Caring That Enables* have had one person who served as coordinator or team leader. The

Project Coordinator recruits volunteers for the parish family ministry team, and facilitates the four training sessions. (See "Tasks and Qualifications for the Project Coordinator" below.)

This person may be a regular team member, or simply serve as resource facilitator to the family ministry team. For example, a parish staff person (DRE, pastoral associate, etc.) may not have the time to be a committed team member, but may serve as project coordinator. Facilitating just the four training sessions may be an attractive option. Most of the parish teams I have facilitated were comprised solely of volunteer parishioners, and received some support and assistance from one member of the parish staff.

A volunteer parishioner may also serve as project coordinator. All the necessary instructions and materials are contained in the manual. The instructions for each strategy are unique, but simple and straightforward. This person should fulfill the qualifications and requirements for project coordinator.

Tasks and Qualifications for the Project Coordinator

The project coordinator is the most important person for successfully implementing *Caring That Enables*. This person should be selected carefully. He or she should demonstrate the following characteristics, and communicate confidence that he or she can carry out the following tasks.

Qualifications:
- At least one year's experience in volunteering for some area of parish ministry.
- Demonstrated desire to coordinate the *Caring That Enables* project.
- Demonstrated dependability.
- Strong organizational skills.
- Ability to communicate concepts and ideas to a small group of volunteers.
- Demonstrated leadership potential and skills.
- Capacity for creativity and adaptability.

Tasks:
- Must agree to serve as project coordinator for one year.
- Must read and study the entire *Caring That Enables* manual.

- Must take primary responsibility for recruiting volunteers to serve on the parish family ministry team.
- Must organize and facilitate the orientation session for *Caring That Enables*.
- Must organize and facilitate the four training sessions.
- May serve as a member/leader of the parish family ministry team.

Selecting the Volunteer Team

Recruiting volunteers for service in the church is an art. Some are rough and crude in their artistic expression. Others are more refined. The teams who have succeeded with *Caring That Enables* have done well recruiting and selecting their volunteers. The teams that failed did a poor job putting their team together. I cannot over-emphasize the importance of this step.

In my experience of ministry, I have succeeded in securing volunteers when I keep several points in mind.

- Look for "natural leaders" who have a genuine desire to serve family life in the parish, and are willing to take responsibility for the tasks involved. Natural leaders are dependable, and usually have good communication skills.
- Look for "successful transitioners": people who have grown through stresses of family transition (e.g. newlywed to developing family, newly divorced to single lifestyle).
- Look for folks to fill out the diversity of your team. Ideally, the parish family ministry team should have members representing a variety of family forms.
- Use a personal approach to recruit team members. One-to-one personal contact always works best.
- Be specific about what you are asking them to do. How much time is involved? How many meetings? How much extra work? How long must I be committed? etc. Provide a job description.
- Name the person's gifts and talents. Assure him or her that you believe he or she can do the job. Many people do not volunteer because they feel inadequate. Some sincere flattery can go a long way.

- Always give the person a chance to say "no." People who say "yes" reluctantly make lousy volunteers.
- Provide the necessary orientation for new team members.
- Provide all necessary materials, handouts and resources for new team members. Note: all of these are contained in this manual.

After the first team is formed, it should become the responsibility of all team members to recruit new members as needed.

Orientation Session

Perhaps the most helpful step in recruiting team members is sponsoring an orientation/information session for potential volunteers. This session introduces the strategies and process for *Caring That Enables,* allowing prospective volunteers to hear what is involved before committing themselves.

Chapter I provides a good outline for the orientation meeting. This material covers the basic goals and steps in the project. Present this information to those who attend. Give each person a copy of the Parish Family Ministry Team Member Job Description (Handout II.1). Also, describe the general schedule of the four training sessions (see below). Be sure to allow plenty of time for questions.

Use more than just the parish bulletin to let people know about the orientation session. Extend a personal invitation to those who you think would be good team members. Tell them it is purely an informational meeting. Attending the session does not commit them to serving on the family ministry team.

HANDOUT II.1

PARISH FAMILY MINISTRY TEAM MEMBER
JOB DESCRIPTION

Goal: The goal of the parish family ministry team is to enrich the quality of family life in the parish using three specific strategies for parish family ministry: family life awareness raising, family sensitivity in parish ministry, and focus and invite.

Who: The family ministry team will consist of five to eight volunteer parishioners. A parish staff person may serve on the team, but it is not essential.

Responsibilities: Each volunteer team member agrees to . . .
- Serve on the parish family ministry team for one year.
- Attend all four training sessions.
- Meet with fellow team members approximately once a month, and carry out individual tasks related to the strategies for family ministry.
- Work with fellow team members in implementing the three strategies of parish family ministry. All the necessary steps are outlined in the four training sessions.
- Provide progress reports to parish leadership. Collaboration with pastor, parish staff and pastoral council is essential.

Qualifications: The volunteer team member should . . .
- Be concerned about the quality of family life in today's church and society.
- Be able to work with other volunteers in a team setting.
- Be open to learning and trying new things.
- Be dependable.

Dates for Training Sessions

After several years of experimenting, I found that the best times for training sessions are...

Orientation Meeting............late spring or early fall
Training Session #1 ....early fall
Training Session #2 ....early fall (two or three weeks later)
Training Session #3 ....sometime in January
Training Session #4 ....late spring

Let me explain this timing and sequence.

The orientation session, as you know, is used to help recruit team members. If your parish normally recruits volunteers in the spring, that would be the best time to have the orientation session. However, most parishes wait until early fall to do volunteer recruiting. If this is your case, it is more appropriate to have this meeting in the fall.

Training sessions #1 and #2 go together well. At the first session, team members learn the strategy of Family Life Awareness Raising. This strategy is ongoing, and the team can begin implementing it immediately after the training.

Within a couple of weeks, they are then ready to learn the strategy of Bringing a Family Sensitivity to Parish Ministry, which is covered in Training Session #2. This too is an ongoing strategy, but initial development will likely require a couple of months.

Early or mid-January is a good time for Training Session #3—learning the strategy of Focus and Invite. This strategy takes at least two and a half months to carry out. The Focus and Invite Gathering is the culmination of this strategy and should not happen too late in the spring. My experience with parishes has been that after the end of April the turnout for the gathering is usually lower than desired. They are better off to postpone it until the next fall.

Training Session #4 works best in the late spring, or anytime soon after the Focus and Invite Gathering. This session is designed primarily to be an assessment of progress for the team and planning for the future. This session also provides a good opportunity for celebrating and affirming the team members.

Inform the Parish

Once you have a parish family ministry team, use the regular channels of communication in the parish (bulletin, newsletter, pulpit, etc.) to inform parishioners about the training they will receive, and the services they will perform. Ask the parish to pray for families and family ministry.

Family life can now be a priority in your parish. Take advantage of opportunities to keep parishioners informed about family ministry. This effort might even lead to one or two more volunteers.

Additional Hints

A few additional things you should keep in mind while implementing *Caring That Enables* are . . .

• Be visible and vocal. Let the parish know what the team is doing. They will be pleased that a group of people care enough to try to make a difference for families.

• Always communicate with your pastor. Give him summaries of the training sessions and your regular team meetings. Whether or not he has time or interest to be involved with the family ministry team, he will appreciate knowing what you are up to. Do this in a way that exonerates any guilt he might feel for not participating in team meetings or gatherings. Pastors cannot possibly attend every parish meeting. Make sure he is invited, but let him know he is not obligated.

• Remember, *something* in family ministry is better than nothing. Even if your endeavors are less than perfect, at least it is a legitimate, genuine effort. People will appreciate it.

III Training Session #1

Family Life Awareness Raising

As a mother of three young children, Ellen is concerned about the atmosphere of permissiveness and instant gratification they are exposed to. She believes strongly in traditional family values (the permanence of marriage, parents as key educators of their children, etc.), but society seems to have compromised those values.

Ellen was particularly critical of divorced persons until her best friend recently separated from her husband. After hearing the whole story, Ellen could then see that some relationships are flawed from the beginning and a break-up is inevitable.

She still believes in strong marriage and family values, but has learned to embrace folks whose life experience has been different from hers. Ellen and her friend spend much time together growing and learning from each other.

How does your parish embrace and call forth the gifts of those living in non-traditional family forms? At the same time, how does your parish communicate traditional marriage and family values? Does your parish help parishioners recognize both the strengths and the woundedness of all households? These are the key questions at the heart of the strategy of Family Life Awareness Raising.

This training session has four main parts. First, since this is the first training session, it's important to begin with a warm welcome and adequate orientation. Try to create an informal atmosphere. Providing refreshments will help. If team members do not know each other well, some introduction exercises are suggested below.

Second, the project coordinator will give a brief presentation on "Social Change and the Family." The purpose here is to raise awareness among team members of the realities of marriage and family life today. The material presented is generally focused on household life in America. The team's discussion should try to filter this material through the realities of your particular community.

Third, the team will learn the steps of Family Life Awareness Raising—implementing the strategy. They will learn how to use the tools of communication in the parish to raise consciousness among all parishioners of the realities of marriage and family life. The church has always been faithful at proclaiming the ideals and values of family living, but has not always recognized the realities of household living and tied them into the spiritual life of the parish. Here the team will also see how other parishes have done family life awareness raising.

The session concludes with time for the team to begin planning their own awareness raising. They will talk about which channels of communication would be best to use. Time will probably not allow the team to finish planning, but they should get a good start. Before the closing prayer, be sure to determine the date and place of your next meeting.

For the Project Coordinator

Proper preparation for the first training session is essential. Prior to the meeting you will need to do the following tasks:

1. Notify team members of the date, time and place for the training session.

2. Reserve (if necessary) and prepare the meeting room. Participants should be seated comfortably in a circle or semi-circle. You may want to have a chalkboard or flip-chart for your presentation on "Social Change and the Family."

3. Read the entire lesson plan for this session (all of Chapter III). Make whatever adjustments you think are warranted.

4. Make enough copies of each handout—one per team member. You may want to provide a folder or binder for each person to keep notes and handouts from all the training sessions.

5. Read and study the information on "Social Change and the Family." Prepare a presentation that communicates this material to the team. You may simply read it to them or give a presentation in your own words. Either way, it is important for the team to hear this information and discuss it together.

6. Prepare the opening and closing prayers. For each training session you will find two scripture passages and a theme statement for prayer. Use this material to create suitable prayer experiences for your team. You may wish to use one reading for the opening prayer and the other for the closing prayer. Perhaps you will want to use them both at the beginning and the end. Perhaps you will have only one prayer/reflection time. It's up to you. I encourage you to involve other team members in the prayers.

7. Arrange for desired refreshments.

Once these tasks are completed, you are ready for the first training session.

Training Session Outline

I. Getting Started   (allow 20 minutes)
   A. Welcome
   B. Introductions
   C. Orientation
   D. Prayer

II. Social Change and the Family   (allow 30 minutes)
   A. Presentation
   B. Group Discussion

III. The Strategy of Family Life Awareness Raising   (45 minutes)
   A. Explanation of Strategy (handouts)
   B. Variations by Other Parishes
   C. Implications for Family Spirituality
   D. Group Questions and Discussion

IV. Team Planning   (allow 45 minutes)
   A. Team Decides How To Implement Strategy
   B. *Who* Will Do *What* by *When?*

V. Conclusion   (allow 10 minutes)
   A. Date, Time and Place for Next Team Meeting
   B. Notification for Training Session #2
   C. Closing Prayer

Getting Started

Welcome. The project coordinator should do everything possible to make each team member feel welcome and comfortable. Coffee and cookies or some sort of snack always helps. You should call the meeting to order with words of welcome and a brief general statement about the purpose for gathering: to learn strategies for parish family ministry.

Introductions. Go around the group and ask each team member to introduce himself or herself. Use the discussion questions below to help them get to know each other and begin building community.

1. What is one personal trait you have inherited from your family of origin (your parents, brothers and sisters)?
2. What is one personal trait that one of your children has inherited from you?

These questions have never failed to stimulate discussion at the first training session, even among folks who have never met.

Orientation. After introductions, give a brief overview of this first training session. Use the outline above to let team members know what will be covered. Be sure to nuance the outline according to whatever adjustments you have made.

Opening Prayer. The prayer theme for this session is "God Has Called You To Serve." The scripture readings emphasize the posture and attitude we must have in order to serve God's families. These readings are Matthew 5:13-16 and Colossians 3:12-17. In this prayer experience, team members should be encouraged in some way to dedicate their service to God. They should also be affirmed in their desire to minister.

Social Change in the Family

The text below attempts to sensitize team members to some realities that families face today. Then, through the strategy of family life awareness raising, they will attempt to sensitize parishioners.

Presentation. In a manner comfortable to you, communicate the information below.

The portrait of American family life is much different from what we were raised to believe it should be. The family is changing at a rapid pace. This is not the first time family life has changed. It has often shifted its structure and function in response to changes occurring in society. Before now, however, society has never experienced such rapid change. The result: families struggle to keep up. They encounter issues and difficulties with greater frequency and intensity.

What are the issues that today's families encounter?

• *Divorce.* The United States is the most marrying country in the world. A higher percentage of adults get married in the U.S. than in any other country. We are also the most divorcing country in the world, and the most remarrying. Sadly, second marriages are failing at a faster rate than first marriages.

Divorce has created several family forms that are now common throughout American society.

• *Single-Parent Families.* By the time our children graduate from high school a large number of them will have lived or are living in a one-parent household. These families face many challenges: finding quality child care, effective meal planning, balancing work and family and "me" time. The greatest challenge is family finances. Divorce nearly always means a decreased income for women, and most single-parent families are headed by women. Often the only way she can increase her income is to remarry.

• *Blended Families.* Gone are the days of the "typical American family" as a working father, stay-at-home mother, a couple of children, a dog and a station wagon. Blended and single-parent families now outnumber never divorced families.

Blended families deal with a myriad of issues for parents and children: higher marital expectations, adjusting to a "new" parent and siblings, child visitation patterns, maintaining the appropriate relationship with the ex-spouse, maintaining contact with the children's grandparents. Extended family relationships are incredibly complex in blended families.

• *Two-Earner Families.* The phenomenon of women employed outside the home is one of the most drastic changes our society has experienced in this century. It has affected sex roles, cultural norms and activity patterns that were firmly entrenched in our society less than a generation ago.

Some women work outside the home for their own personal and professional self-fulfillment, others out of financial necessity. Many women are the sole earners in the household. The multi-million dollar industry of child care in our country is directly related to this issue.

Women encounter several problems in the work force that most men do not. First, they cannot make as much money. On average, women make less money for comparable work than men. Furthermore, the higher paying jobs are less available to women. This problem is greatly intensified for minority women.

Another problem stems from the fact that women remain the primary "nurturer" in most homes. Household roles and responsibilities have shifted to accommodate two earner families, but women still have the lion's share of family responsibility around the house. In effect, the woman often carries the load of two full-time jobs. Add to this the not uncommon circumstance of caring for an elderly parent, and you've got a prime candidate for parent burnout.

For those women not employed outside the home, they often feel socially inferior. In many sectors we no longer value the homemaker and mother. We expect her to have a "profession" as well.

• *Family Size.* Households have shrunk steadily in the last one hundred years until now the average is just under three persons per household. This is a result of American mobilization, not effective methods of birth control.

There was a time when children were an asset to the productivity and survival of the family. During that time nearly all major social functions were carried out in a family or small community setting: health care, education, religious formation, socialization, recreation, work, etc. The more family members in the house or nearby, the easier it was to carry out these functions.

Today many social institutions have usurped the family in providing these services. Beginning with the age of industrialization, families moved from the farm to the city, adults (mostly men) left home to do their jobs, and thus arose the human services industry.

Along with industrialization came mobilization. It is much simpler to move a two generation household of four than a three generation household of eight or more. And so the family unit has shrunk. One of the consequences of this phenomenon is the increased burden of child rearing for parents, especially the mother. In many homes she carries nearly the entire load of raising the children. No other culture in the world places so much responsibility on one person.

• *Aging.* The four generation family is now the norm in the United States. This is ironic when you consider that for many families these generations do not live anywhere near each other. The result: the elderly feel isolated and alone, adults are overburdened worrying and caring for both a younger and an older generation, and children cannot remember their grandparents and great-grandparents because they don't see them often enough.

• *Family Crises*. On top of all this, statistics show a great increase in acute family problems: poverty, alcohol and drug dependency, sexual and other forms of abuse, runaway children, teen pregnancy, suicide, etc. Part of the increase is due to better record keeping and a greater willingness to admit problems and seek help, but these problems are real and they are increasing.

• *In Our Community*. Given the unique situations of our parish and community, what family issues and crises haven't I mentioned? How are our families challenged to cope with the struggles and realities that today's society presents?

Conclusion. From this description of American family life, some will conclude that it is just a matter of time before it disintegrates. What do you think? Is the family dying?

The family is not dying, but it is struggling with "changing pains." The family has always shifted its functions and structure according to changes occurring in society. The difficulty for families today is keeping up with a rapidly changing society. Keep in mind, however, that it is not just families who need society. Society itself cannot survive without families. Family life is a foundational institution. And so healthier families make a healthier society.

We also know the family is the most adaptable institution of society. It continually shifts its structure and roles in order to co-exist with all other aspects of the human community.

The church is challenged to embrace the full realities of family life today. The church is in a unique position to help families deal with their changing pains. Can we ease their difficult transitions from one stage to the next and provide a buffer of support as they are bombarded by the challenges of society? Most of the information above is probably not new to you. Yet so many of us, when in the context of our parish or church, hold onto that old stereotype of the "traditional" family.

There is a difference between family values and family form. Of course we want to uphold traditional Catholic family values, including the permanence of marriage, parents as primary educators of children, marriage as a reflection of Christ's love for his people, etc. Yet today's reality finds many households in something other than the traditional family form.

We must embrace all forms of family life. We must genuinely receive their weaknesses and woundedness. Indeed, aren't we all wounded in one way or another? We must also challenge households, regardless of form, to share their gifts and strengths with the community. Think of what we could learn from single-parent families about effective meal planning, finding quality child care and other related issues. All families have strengths and healthy traits. I believe they can share their strengths with others in the parish to enhance the quality of family life for all. And, finally, we must challenge all families regardless of form to uphold traditional Christian values of love and acceptance of all God's people.

Group Discussion. The project coordinator should allow time for team members to discuss the information presented. These discussion starters may help focus the dialogue:

- Of the issues mentioned above, the one that affects our family the most is . . .
- Of the issues mentioned above, the ones that affect our parish community the most are . . .
- The level of awareness among our parishioners of these family issues is . . .
- If our parishioners were made more aware of these issues and how they impact the parish, they would . . .

This material often provokes a lot of feelings, opinions and questions.

The Strategy of Family Life Awareness Raising

Strategy Explained. As mentioned, the team will learn how to use the tools of communication in the parish to raise awareness of the realities of family life. They may choose to have a corner in the parish bulletin on a regular basis. They may choose to write prayers of the faithful for Sunday mass, or write an article for the parish newsletter, or use notes sent home from school. All of these are viable avenues for awareness raising and have been used by other parish teams.

The goal of awareness raising is to give folks some interesting thoughts and information about family life. You are not asking anyone to volunteer for anything or to come to any program. It is just a piece of information, and it is free.

The most commonly used approach is the parish bulletin. Parish teams arrange to have a small corner of space in the bulletin on a regular basis (every other week or once a month). In this space the team provides interesting information pertaining to family life issues: statistics, tips for parents, quotes from influential persons, etc. Similarly, several teams have arranged to write the Sunday prayers of the faithful on a regular basis.

Material for "awareness raisers" is abundant. Stay alert for articles in newspapers, magazines and other news media. Even one simple quote, statistic or perhaps a cartoon can form the basis for a good awareness raiser. When you find something interesting, cut it out and save it until it can be used. Don't limit yourselves to purely religious literature. Family concerns make the secular news nearly every day. You'll be amazed at what you can find in your daily paper and/or weekly news magazines.

Awareness raisers should be short and to the point. A combination of a national statistic followed by a sentence or two on how this information applies to your parish works quite well. The examples below appeared in Sunday bulletins. Tips, ideas and anecdotes about parenting and family life also make good awareness raisers.

HANDOUT III.1

SAMPLE AWARENESS RAISERS

• "Many service institutions are showing a renewed interest in family life and how to provide their services in ways that support families' own responsibilities. For example, health care institutions over the last years have made notable innovations, such as hospices for dying persons and opportunities for family participation in birthing.
   For more information, call . . ."

• "'In the public arena, conservatives and liberals are moving toward the consensus that family concerns should be front and center of the public policymaking process. For the first time, policymakers are talking about injecting a family perspective into public policy and human services.'
—G. Gallop, *American Families*.
   For more information, please call . . ."

• "Because women are employed outside the home, the vast majority of families today are required to negotiate and adjust roles and family responsibilities within the home. The previous generation clearly defined the roles of wife and husband, mother and father. Today, each family must define these roles and responsibilities for itself. While this can be seen as an opportunity, it is also a serious source of stress for many families.
   For more information call . . ."

• "Jesus said, 'Who is my mother? Who are my brothers?' Then, extending his hand toward his disciples, he said, 'There are my mother and my brothers. Whoever does the will of my heavenly Father is brother and sister and mother to me.' —Matt. 12:48-50
   St. Mary's Parish has more than 450 families."

• "When it comes to educating children, parents are the first teachers and the most influential. Thus, it is important that effective teaching styles are developed by parents. A recent edition of NETWORK for Public Schools carried an opening article on 'Effective Families Help Children Succeed in School.' They listed several characteristics of effective families.

1. They have a feeling of control over their lives.
2. They have frequent communication of high expectations to children.
3. They have a family dream of success for the future.
4. Hard work is viewed as a key to success.
5. They have an active, not sedentary, lifestyle.

What 'strengths' do you have in your family? What areas do you need to work on?"

• "I've yet to meet anyone who chose family over career and regretted it. No one on his deathbed ever said, 'I didn't spend enough time with my business.'"—Paul Tsongas, on leaving the U.S. Senate.

A couple of tips regarding this strategy are in order. First, be consistent and ongoing with your awareness raising. In doing so, you will build credibility for yourselves as a family ministry team. Over time, you may help shift the posture of the parish toward a better relationship with family life.

Second, be sure to go through proper parish channels for using bulletin space and providing Sunday prayers of the faithful. In some parishes the office secretary screens everything that goes into the bulletin, while the pastor may perform that job in other parishes. In *every* parish there is a deadline for submitting material for the Sunday bulletin. What are the procedures in your parish? Similar care should be taken with Sunday prayers of the faithful. Be sure the prayers are placed in the hands of the right person (not necessarily the pastor) in plenty of time before the first weekend mass.

Variations by Other Parishes. In addition to parish bulletin announcements, there is much room for creativity with this strategy. The examples below should help your team determine the best way to implement this strategy in your parish.

HANDOUT III.2

VARIATIONS ON AWARENESS RAISING

• *Awareness Raising with the Pastor.* One team occasionally gave articles about family issues to their pastor. They included a little note, "Dear Father, We thought you might find this interesting. Perhaps you could work it into a homily sometime." The team had a good relationship with their pastor, and so they could do this without putting undue pressure on him. This technique might also be used with other staff members.

• *Sunday Prayers of the Faithful.* Several teams have arranged to write these prayers on a regular basis. Some examples include:

"We pray for parents and teenagers, that they can live together in harmony during these often turbulent years."

"We pray for all ecumenical couples, that they appreciate the richness of their two faith experiences."

• *Parish Newsletter.* One parish arranged to have a regular column in their parish quarterly newsletter. The awareness raisers were longer than other examples, but appropriate for the publication.

• *More on Awareness Raisers in the Bulletin.* Several teams have developed a logo representing family/household life that accompanies their bulletin messages. The logo catches the eye of parishioners and draws attention to the awareness raiser. One team ran its messages two consecutive weeks, figuring that some folks would have missed it the first time around.

Implications for Family Spirituality

At first glance this strategy may not seem to have much impact on the spiritual lives of families. Yet family spirituality is tied directly to overall family health. Therefore, if a parish communicates a posture of interest and support for family health, then families will be more open to the spiritual and apostolic opportunities in the parish.

One goal of awareness raising is to communicate that your parish cares for and tries to understand the joys and struggles of everyday family life. Of course the parish is interested in spiritual growth, but that cannot be separated from the crazy chaos of household living.

When families perceive this genuine care, understanding and support, they will be more open to the spiritual values the parish can offer. The first priority of parish family ministry is *not* helping families be better Catholics. Rather, it is helping and challenging them to discover their own strengths to be healthy families. If the parish can do this, families will also be better Christians.

Discussion. Take a few minutes to discuss any questions or comments team members may have.

Team Planning

Implementing the Strategy. The team now decides how they wish to implement the strategy of family life awareness raising. Look back through the information and handouts. Which technique is best for your parish? Be sure to outline the particular action steps. Be specific and detailed in your planning. With each step, answer this question: "*Who* will do *what* by *when*?" If there is not enough time for planning at the first training session, set a date, time and place for your team to meet again. After your team gets into a pattern of ongoing awareness raising, one or two team members should be able to keep the strategy going. Strategizing for awareness raising should take place before the team experiences Training Session #2.

Conclusion

The project coordinator informs the team when Training Session #2 will take place. Any last minute questions or details can also be dealt with at this time.

Closing Prayer. Recall the prayer theme and scripture readings for this session. Theme "God Has Called You To Serve." Readings: Matthew 5:13-16 and Colossians 3:12-17.

IV
Training Session #2

Bringing a Family Sensitivity to Parish Ministry

Someone from the Jorgenson household could attend a meeting at St. James Parish every night of the week. The Jorgensons are perhaps more active and committed in their parish than the average Catholic family. (Except, of course, Erica, 11, who can't stand CCD anymore and will do anything to get out of going on Tuesday nights.) Yet, in spite of their faithful commitment, as spring approaches they are feeling a bit stressed and fragmented. Oh, they don't actually make it to a meeting every night of the week, but there's always that feeling of "should." If only there were a night of the week with no parish activities.

How does your parish impact family living? How does your parish honor the "church of the home"? How does your parish advocate for families and households in the wider community? How does your parish help families deal with the change and growth in individuals that parish programs encourage? These are the key questions for this training session of bringing family sensitivity to parish ministry.

The best parishes have the most activities, right? Not so. Many parishes have so many programs that families like the Jorgensons are fragmented each week trying to fulfill their commitments to such things as scouting, sacramental preparation, youth group, *RENEW* group, Bible study, etc. One could attend a meeting at the parish center every night of the week, and some folks do.

Yet how can that be good for family life? Quality family life comes from quality *and quantity* time together. A parish cannot

35

force families to enjoy each other, but it can take a look at how it might be preventing them from doing so.

A family sensitivity in parish ministry means looking for simple adjustments in existing programs and services that will enrich family and household life instead of fragmenting it. It can also mean helping families in their relationships with other institutions that hinder their family living—i.e. health care, schools, recreation, job, etc.

In a word, this session attempts to help us do all we can for families *without creating new parish programs*. It might even help your parish cut back on some of its activities. Imagine that! A night at the parish with nothing going on! That's what some parish teams have succeeded in doing. They convinced the parish pastoral council to declare one night a week as family night. No parish meetings or sessions could take place on that night, and families were encouraged to spend the evening together. The family ministry team even provided age-appropriate suggestions for how they might spend that time together.

Other parishes have worked to give parents more involvement in their children's education programs, as well as bridge the family experience at home with the religious experience at church. Numerous examples of how to bring a family sensitivity to parish ministry are provided in this session. It's up to you and your team to figure out the best course of action. Read on. You'll learn all about it.

For the Project Coordinator

During this session, parish team members will be introduced to a variety of ways of bringing a family sensitivity to parish ministry. As project coordinator, you will present some theory and background information on this concept of ministry. The team will then hear how other parish family ministry teams have worked with this strategy, and its implications for family spirituality. They will then be ready to plan their own implementation.

Preparations for this training session are basically the same as for Training Session #1. See the list of tasks for the project coordinator in Chapter III. After reading the entire lesson plan (Chapter IV), you will want to prepare your presentation on "Family Perspective in Parish Ministry." Be sure to make copies of all handouts for the team members. You will also need to prepare the prayer experiences for this session. The theme and scripture reading are listed below.

Training Session Outline

I. Welcome, Orientation and Prayer   (allow 15 minutes)

II. Family Perspective in Parish Ministry   (allow 40 minutes)
- What does it mean?
- What does it seek to do?

   A. Presentation by Project Coordinator
   B. Group Discussion with Handouts

III. Examples of Parish Implementation   (allow 20 minutes)
   A. Review Implementation Ideas
   B. Group Discussion

IV. Implications for Family Spirituality   (allow 20 minutes)
   A. Review Article
   B. Group Discussion

V. Team Planning and Strategizing   (allow 45 minutes)
- *Who* will do *what* by *when*?

VI. Conclusion   (allow 10 minutes)
   A. Next Team Meeting
   B. Next Training Session
   C. Closing Prayer

Welcome, Orientation and Prayer

Welcome. The project coordinator welcomes each team member back for Training Session #2. The focus of this session is bringing a family sensitivity to parish ministry: learning how to work with other ministries and services in the parish and helping them incorporate a family perspective.

Orientation. The project coordinator gives an orientation to this session by stating the purpose of the session and reviewing the outline above. As in the previous session, be sure to communicate any adjustments you have made.

Opening Prayer. The prayer theme for this session is "Jesus' Warmth and Hospitality." The scripture reading is John 21:1-14.

Only one reading is chosen because this is a very rich gospel story. I encourage you to use it at both the beginning and the end of the session. You will also find references to this passage in the midst of this chapter.

Family Perspective in Parish Ministry

Presentation. Using the material written below, the project coordinator gives a presentation introducing team members to this important concept in ministry.

"No plan of organized pastoral work at any level must ever fail to take into consideration the pastoral area of the family." This statement by Pope John Paul II in *Familiaris Consortio* captures the meaning of family perspective in a nutshell. Family sensitivity in parish ministry implies looking at a variety of services through the lens of household life, and asking, "What adjustments can be made to be more responsive to the issues and realities that families face today?"

More specifically, a family perspective seeks to do three things.

1. It seeks to sensitize those who serve *families* as to the realities of marriage and family life today. This is just what the strategy of family life awareness raising seeks to accomplish. It is, in effect, a family perspective strategy.

Most parish leaders are aware of family situations today—divorce, single-parenting, dual income, blended, etc. Yet, often there are parish programs which fail to reflect these realities. For example, a catechist was preparing youngsters for first eucharist. In one of her lessons she likened communion to a family meal. She built her entire lesson around the analogy that going to communion at mass is like sitting down with your whole family for an evening meal. She was receiving "glazed" looks from the children. They weren't making the connection. So she interrupted her lesson and asked the children how often they have a meal together with their whole family. Fewer than half experienced a family meal on a regular basis. When she probed further, she found that a good number of the children often fixed their own meal and ate alone in front of the TV. Obviously she had to rework her teaching about eucharist.

What can a parish family ministry team do to help situations like this? As one example, a parish team assisted the catechists in their knowledge and understanding of the family situation of their students. Each teacher received from the team a family information sheet indicating such things as which students came from single-parent or blended families, which came from dual income, which were oldest or youngest in the family, etc. With this information the catechist could tailor the lessons according to family patterns and/or particular family situations.

2. A family perspective seeks to sensitize those who serve the *individual* to broaden their perspective by looking at the individual through the prism of family. When parish ministry brings change (via spiritual growth) to the lives of individuals, families are impacted by that change. One of the most important principles of family systems theory states that if one member of the family system changes, all other members must adjust otherwise the change won't last. What is the primary goal of many ministries in the parish? To bring about change and growth in the lives of individuals. To help them discover God's gracious activity in their lives *and respond to it.* The church must help families with those adjustments.

In such ministries as RCIA and youth group, as well as others, it is necessary and appropriate to focus on the individual, providing an atmosphere for persons to discover a relationship with Christ. This is what evangelization and catechesis are all about. This is why parishes sponsor retreats, service projects, evenings of prayer and reflection, sacramental programs, etc., and it all implies change in the lives of individuals.

Yet what happens *at home* when a person changes and grows in his or her faith? Believe it or not, families will likely resist that change even if it is good. Why? Remember the principle of family systems theory stating that one person's change upsets the balance of the entire system and that families will naturally resist anything that shifts their balance. Therefore a family will often unconsciously work to undo the change that has been encouraged through the ministry program. Therefore, helping families adjust to change and to find a new balance will enrich family life and enhance parish ministry at the same time.

This adjustment does not mean that the whole family must experience the same "conversion" or faith growth, but they must make room for changed individuals to be different than they were before. Families who have an ongoing support structure are usually more successful in finding a new balance than those who are isolated from others.

Parishes, therefore, are challenged to provide support networks that help families adjust to the growth and change in individuals as a result of parish ministry. How can they do that? The logical way is to actively involve family members in the program. Yet this is not always possible. It's hard to imagine, for example, teens being very enthused about parents attending all youth group gatherings, to say nothing about little brothers and sisters.

A more feasible way to assist this transition is to create "bridger experiences" between the program at church and daily life at home. This is where the family ministry team plays a role. For example, one team worked with the parish RCIA program in providing catechumens with simple take-home ideas to share with their families, based on the learning and growth they were experiencing. Another parish team worked with the youth group leaders in creating a "re-entry" session for parents after youth retreats. This gave parents ideas on how they might react to their euphoric teens upon their return home. These "bridger experiences" attempt to connect the work of ministry in the parish to the delicate balance of household life.

3. A family perspective seeks to help families become better *partners* with the many social institutions they deal with regularly (church, school, health care, employer, etc.). Parishes are challenged in two ways here.

First, they must look at their own relationships with families and households. What is the level of partnership between families and the parish? By that I mean: How are the rhythms and dynamics of everyday family life considered in planning, implementing and evaluating parish programs? When parishes over-schedule with too many activities, they fragment family life. When parishes schedule meetings and liturgies only during prime family time, they fragment family life. When parishes create small groups for faith sharing and disciple-making, i.e. parish renewal groups, they sometimes forget that families themselves can be primary faith groups. Again, these efforts are not inherently bad. They are necessary for the life and vitality of the Christian community, and families need a vital Christian community. Yet parishes must be challenged to look at their community building efforts through a family lens and to make appropriate adjustments.

Second, parishes are challenged to advocate for families in their relationships with other institutions and services in society. Service agencies in the community are not deliberately anti-family, but sometimes there are so many procedures, steps and red tape to hurdle that receiving the service becomes a stress in itself. The parish can be a collective voice for families and households in the community.

Today, a key function in family life is *coordinating* the family's relationships with these various programs and services: job, school, doctor's office, little league, dance lessons, scouting. They are all good things, but we all know the kind of juggling act that many parents must endure. A supportive parish community can help folks determine their priorities, say "no" to some things, and speak up for their family concerns.

To conclude, I would like to point out two common myths regarding parish ministry and the family.

1. "A leader's commitment to the parish automatically implies a commitment to the families of the parish." Not necessarily so. Some parish leaders unconsciously take a competitive approach to ministry programming. This means that they *compete* for time on parish and family calendars for their programs and activities. They *compete* for volunteer time and energy. They must be challenged to move toward a *cooperative* approach which attempts to work within the realities and rhythms of household living.

2. "Effective ministry to individuals automatically implies good ministry to the families of those individuals." Again, not necessarily true. In fact, sometimes ministry to individuals happens at the expense of quality family life. When families are fragmented three or four nights a week driving children of various ages to youth group, religious education and sacramental preparation, then these families are hardly enriched by these efforts toward individuals.

In response to these myths, there is one truth which remains constant throughout all areas of service in the church. If we bring a family sensitivity to a particular ministry, it will not only enrich family life, but it will also enhance the quality of that ministry. Therefore, it is in the parish leader's best interest to pursue a family sensitivity.

Group Discussions with Handouts. The handouts below give two ways for parish ministers to evaluate their programs through a family lens. Use the first handout to discuss your parish in light of the information presented above.

HANDOUT IV.1

PARISH/FAMILY RELATIONSHIP

The four statements below seek to evaluate the relationship between family life and the parish. They can be adapted for any particular ministry (religious education, youth ministry, RCIA, liturgy, etc.). When leaders of these ministries respond to these statements, they begin to see areas where they can make simple adjustments to be more family sensitive.

Take a few minutes to complete the statements yourself. Share your responses with other team members. Are there any common concerns that surface? Are there any ideas for bringing a family perspective to the parish?

• Our parish hinders family life when . . .

• Our parish strengthens family life by . . .

• Our families hinder parish life when . . .

• Our families enhance parish life by . . .

HANDOUT IV.2

FAMILY IMPACT STUDY

This sheet is a more detailed questionnaire. It is best used when leaders of a ministry are planning their efforts for the future. If they consider these questions seriously, it ensures that their plans will carry a family sensitivity. The questions below are focused on catechesis, but they can easily be translated to reflect other areas of service in the church.

Your team might consider developing questionnaires like this for leaders in your parish. If approached in the right manner, they will appreciate your concern.

Child Catechesis

• Does your program address only the child's needs, the needs of the child in relation to his or her family, or the overall needs of the entire family?

• What underlying attitudes concerning the family situation are built into your program (e.g. regarding single, blended, dual career families, etc.)?

• Does your program have a process that helps the children and their families deal with the change and growth your program may encourage?

• How are parents involved in your program's planning, implementation and evaluation?

• How does your program improve the capacity for young

families to master the challenging developmental issues of this stage in family life?

• How does your program improve the relationship between the parish and young families?

• What is one immediate adjustment your program can implement to become more family sensitive?

• What is one long term goal your program can incorporate to increase its family sensitivity?

These questions will be valuable for catechists and educators to consider and discuss. Ask them of parents too. They can give more advice than you may want.

Examples of Parish Implementation

Written below is a capsule summary of numerous ways family ministry teams have attempted to bring a family sensitivity to parish ministry. Each effort has been utilized with success in at least one parish setting. Your team may want to adopt one or several of these ideas. Or you may think of new ideas after reading these. The possibilities for family perspective adjustments are endless.

HANDOUT IV.3

IDEAS FOR FAMILY SENSITIVITY

Sunday Liturgy. One parish team approached the liturgy committee with several ideas for making the Sunday liturgy more sensitive to families and children. Some of their ideas included an occasional homily for children, an occasional children's song, and opportunities for families to bring up the gifts. This idea worked well because the family ministry team was not asking for something that takes a lot of energy to accomplish, such as a monthly children's liturgy. Instead they offered simple adjustments in the regular routine of Sunday mass.

Parish Staff. A family ministry team arranged to present several basic ideas about family perspective to the parish staff. Then they conducted a brief goal setting session where the staff had an opportunity to reflect on the ministries they conduct. They were asked to think of one immediate adjustment that could be made in their ministry, and one long term goal to incorporate a family sensitivity.

Parish Family Night. One team approached the parish council and asked them to declare one night of the week to be "Family Night." This meant that no parish activities would take place on that night, and families would be encouraged to spend that evening together. The family ministry team also provided occasional resources and ideas for families to spend that time together.

Community Family Night. Another team collaborated with other churches in their small town and approached the local public school board to declare one night a week where there were no school activities, games, practices, or concerts. After succeeding, some churches in town used that evening as "church night." At the insistence of the family ministry team, the Catholic parish shared those nights with families. The parish used half the evenings for their programs, and encouraged families to spend the other evenings at home.

Parish Council Advocate. Several parish teams have approached their parish council and requested that a member of the council be appointed "family advocate." This person's role is to challenge the council, when considering any decision, to ask, "How will this decision impact family life in the parish?" The advocate does not necessarily need particular expertise or knowledge in family related issues. He or she simply has to be a persistent question raiser.

Youth Group Parent Survey. A family life committee worked with youth group volunteers to create a parallel parent need survey for the youth program. This meant that in addition to surveying young people on the topics they wished to address, a similar survey was given to parents of teens allowing them to give input to the youth program as well.

Youth Group Parent Advisory Group. One parish team worked with the youth program leaders to develop a parent advisory group. This group allowed parents to provide input to the youth program without having to attend youth meetings or chaperone dances, etc. The role of the advisory group was to help the youth minister and volunteers choose the best ways to meet the needs of teens and their families. A similar group could also be created for religious education in the parish.

Youth Group Retreat Re-Entry. A parish team worked with the youth leaders to create a re-entry session for parents of teens following the youth group retreat. This involved a simple meeting with parents, giving them ideas and suggestions for how they might interact with their teen when he or she returns from the retreat experience.

Family Sensitivity in Religious Education Classes. One family ministry team worked with catechists, helping them determine the family makeup of each student in the class. If the teacher knows the family background of the students, then she or he can cater the lessons to the life experiences of the young people. The teacher can also avoid making false assumptions related to family and household living.

Parent Involvement in Marriage Preparation. A family ministry team approached the pastor and sponsor couples for marriage preparation and asked them to consider involving parents of the engaged in the preparation process. They did this by establishing that one of the sessions with the priest involve parents and the engaged couple. The focus of this session was on family history and expectations in marriage.

Thank You Notes to Committees and Services. One of the more innovative ideas involved writing acknowledgment notes to various committees in the parish when they did something that was particularly sensitive to family life. This allowed the family ministry team to build a positive relationship with these committees and services and pave the way for suggesting additional ways they might incorporate a family perspective.

Family Perspective in RCIA. A parish team worked on simple, practical take home activities for catechumens based on the learning topics they were introduced to in the RCIA process.

Family Perspective in RENEW and Parish Renewal. A family life committee worked closely with the parish renewal committee helping them make the parish renewal program sensitive to family life. One adjustment allowed for small faith sharing groups to be developed according to the stages of the family life cycle.

These ideas represent a summary of efforts being made in some parishes. There are certainly many other creative ways to seek a family perspective in parish ministry.

Implications for Family Spirituality

This session focuses on the relationship between family life and parish life—perhaps the two most important contributors to faith formation and disciple-making. Ideally, they work together in harmony creating an atmosphere for folks, young and old, to discover God's gracious activity in their lives.

Families need a healthy parish, and parishes need healthy families. When it comes to spiritual enrichment neither can stand alone. Yet at times the partnership is strained. Consider the situation of Alex who is truly growing in his faith. How does this impact his family?

Alex is a catechumen at Sacred Heart Parish. His faith is growing ever deeper, and God is clearly active in his life. He attends several church gatherings each month and is no longer afraid to speak out on issues of injustice. His life has never had such meaning. Yet tension is growing in Alex's family. His cradle-Catholic wife was glad he joined the church, but she had no idea of the impact it would have on him. Alex's children can't understand his zeal for Jesus. He wonders why they cannot accept his change.

This example of how families must deal with change and faith growth is not uncommon. Teens often have a significant faith experience on a retreat. Many college students have a spiritual awakening while involved with the campus Newman Center. Even parents may grow and change while participating in programs like RENEW, Marriage Encounter or Cursillo.

The family is like those mobiles you see hanging from light fixtures—delicately balanced and vulnerable to a sudden gust of wind. Normal life continues as long as the balance of relationships remains constant. But when one member experiences change, the entire family system must adjust. This is not always easy. When we realize that God is active in our homes as well as in the parish, these adjustments are smoother and faith growth is richer for all. Healthy Christian families learn to see God in the ordinary. They can see God in those intimate moments around the birthday dinner table or a cozy embrace in front of the TV. They know too that the face of God will somehow be seen in the tragic moments of a first love lost, or Grandpa's death. All of this is ordinary. All is sacred and holy.

The primary goal of the church is to help individuals grow in their relationship with God. The parish must take some responsibility for the impact of that growth and change on family members. Rather than adjust, Alex's family unconsciously wants to change him back to the way he was. If they have a better understanding of what he is experiencing, and even play a small part in it, their adjustment may be much easier.

When any one of our family members experiences change through faith growth, we can ask parish leaders if programs can be started to help families adjust to the individual's growth. Prayer and sharing experiences at home, for example, can reinforce the catechetical program in the parish. Retreat formats can include a "welcome-back celebration" by families at the end of the weekend. Parents and friends can be asked to write notes of support and prayer that are given to retreatants.

These efforts can serve as a bridge between the faith activity in the parish and that of the home.

Team Planning and Strategizing

Keep in mind that implementing a family perspective in parish ministry can be like the experience of Jesus, the son of a carpenter standing on the shore telling fishermen how to fish (John 21:1-14). If you do not use a little tact, diplomacy and affirmation, you will likely fail. Here are a few guiding steps for your team as you work to implement this strategy.

84717582

HANDOUT IV.4

PRACTICAL STEPS FOR FAMILY SENSITIVITY

Partnering with Another Ministry. As you look at the various ministries in the parish, pick one that you believe fits the following criteria:

- It needs to make some adjustments in order to be more sensitive to families.
- You believe your team can offer some creative suggestions for making those adjustments.
- Leaders of the ministry would welcome your suggestions and be willing to work in partnership with you.

In other words, look for a group that would be interested in adjusting their program to be more family sensitive, and would not be antagonistic if you approached them with some ideas on how to do so.

Meet with the Leaders of the Other Ministry. Make arrangements to meet with the leaders of the chosen ministry. When you meet with them, first affirm the work they are doing. Praise them for the service they provide, and communicate your genuine appreciation. Then share with them some of the learning you have gained around this concept of a family perspective in ministry. Point out that it is not a new program, but rather a new way of looking at ministry in the church—through a family lens.

Explore Together Possible Adjustments. Based on the examples given above, and your own creativity, offer ideas for possible adjustments. You might want to lead them through a process of reflecting on how their ministry impacts family life by using some of the family impact questions. Be sure to communicate your willingness to work with them. This must be a collaborative partnership.

With these suggestions in mind, now it is time for your team to plan how you will implement the strategy of bringing a family sensitivity to parish ministry. Remember, be specific and detailed. Answer the question, *Who* will do *what* by *when?*

Conclusion

Before adjourning, be sure the team has a date, time and place for their next meeting. They will likely need to continue their discussion and planning in order to carry out the first two strategies—awareness raising and family sensitivity.

Also, announce the date, time and place for Training Session #3.

Recall the prayer theme and reading for this session. Theme: "Jesus' Warmth and Hospitality." Reading: John 21:1-14.

V

Training Session #3

Focus and Invite

Sarah and her daughter Amy have been through some rough times in recent years. Sarah's marriage fell apart, and she and Amy have been on their own now for eighteen months. The pain of a broken relationship is somewhat less severe, but the financial burdens seem only to get worse.

But today Sarah feels a little better than usual. Oh sure, the problems are as real as ever, but she's found some folks from her church who understand what she has been through and encourage her to share her woes. You see, they have all been through divorce and single-parenting. They don't often generate many solutions to their problems, but what counts is the soothing experience of sharing stories and being heard. It gives Sarah strength to carry on in these difficult times.

In a simple and do-able way, your team will now learn how to provide similar support experiences for others. During this session they will learn ways to *focus* on a group of parents or families of like-concerns, and *invite* them together for mutual support and ongoing enrichment. This strategy is the closest we come to creating a new parish "program." It is a one night program with possibilities for follow-up. However, the follow-up activities will be designed in a simple and straightforward manner, so they are easily conducted by a small group.

The training session itself involves four primary segments. After the group gathers and prays, the first segment explores the family life cycle. The project coordinator will give a presentation on the developmental stages of family life. This presentation helps the team recognize the common tasks, issues and periods of transition which characterize families at various stages of maturity. The family life cycle provides the rationale and common base for the Focus and Invite strategy. Even though all families are unique, it helps us see how and why nearly all families encounter similar challenges at somewhat predictable times. It also shows how families of similar needs and experiences can benefit from gathering together.

Have you ever seen advertising in your parish bulletin or community newspaper for a series on parenting that reads something like "... featuring Mr. and Mrs. Parenting Expert, who will tell you all you need to know about parenting!! ALL PARENTS SHOULD COME!!" If you're like me, you never feel completely adequate as a parent, so you are likely to be susceptible to this kind of advertising. Of course you want to be a good parent. Yet when you arrive, you realize that your needs as a parent of, say, pre-schoolers are certainly different from the couple next to you who are worried sick about their teens, or the single mother behind you. No matter how good they are, Mr. and Mrs. Parenting Expert cannot meet all those different needs at the same time.

The second segment is a thorough exploration of the focus and invite strategy itself. Nearly all the information is contained in handouts for team members, and so the project coordinator will "walk" the group through them. Each step of the strategy is clearly explained, but feel free to incorporate your own variation. The most useful handout is the "Timeline for Focus and Invite" (Handout V.4). This will become a valuable worksheet for the team as it implements this strategy.

The third segment takes a look at implications for family spirituality. Team members should be reminded of the spiritual context of providing support and encouragement to families of similar needs. Periods of transition and change in the life of a family can provide great opportunities of spiritual healing and growth.

Finally, the team will begin planning for their focus and invite gathering. They will discern which group of families to focus upon and then do preliminary work to prepare for the one night gathering. Be sure to allow some time for the team to start laying the groundwork for implementation. And, of course, set a date and time for the next team meeting.

Nuts and Bolts for the Project Coordinator

Preparation for this session is similar to the first two training sessions. Try to create an atmosphere of warmth and hospitality. Keep in mind that the team has been working on the strategies of awareness raising and family sensitivity. They may need to talk about their progress with these efforts before getting started with the strategy of focus and invite.

As mentioned above, the presentation you will give is on the "family life cycle." All the information is contained in this chapter, and team members will follow along with you on one of their hand-outs. The prayer theme and scripture readings are listed below.

It takes approximately two and a half months to implement this strategy and host a focus and invite gathering. I do not recommend trying to do it more quickly. Each step of the strategy is important and should be done thoroughly. If you are conducting this training session in January or February, you should have no trouble hosting your focus and invite gathering during the early spring. If for some reason your team cannot have the focus and invite session in early spring, I suggest they plan it for the next fall. Why? Other parish teams have learned that focus and invite gatherings are not always well attended during late spring and summer. However, one parish team had their gathering in late May and centered it around summer fun and faith activities for families. It is important to schedule your gathering during an optimal time of the year. Your team will have to judge when that is.

Training Session Outline

I. Welcome, Orientation and Prayer   (allow 10 minutes)

II. Introduction to the Family Life Cycle   (allow 35 minutes)
    A. Presentation
    B. Discussion

III. Implementing Focus and Invite   (allow 45 minutes)
    A. Overview
    B. Determining the Focus Group
    C. Step by Step Instructions and Timeline
    D. Parish Variations to Focus and Invite

IV. Implications for Family Spirituality   (allow 10 minutes)
   A. Review Article
   B. Discussion

V. Team Planning Time   (allow 45 minutes)
   • *Who* Will Do *What* by *When?*

VI. Conclusion
   A. Next Team Meeting and Next Training Session
   B. Closing Prayer

Welcome, Orientation and Prayer

After team members have gathered, the project coordinator should give a brief introduction to this third training session. The outline and information above should suffice. I might suggest a good opening exercise for team members. Ask each person to share about the oldest child and how he or she is impacting the household at this time. From this sharing, your team will likely hear about some of the issues and characteristics of families at various stages of the family life cycle. As explained below, the oldest child normally determines the developmental stage of the family. This discussion leads in well to the presentation on the family life cycle.

Opening Prayer. The prayer theme for this session is "Building a Strong Family Foundation." The scripture readings are Matthew 7:24-27 and Ephesians 2:20-22.

Introduction to the Family Life Cycle

Using the information below, the project coordinator will give a presentation on the family life cycle. As before, present this material in a manner comfortable to you. Reading the text to the team members is O.K.

Presentation. The basis for the focus and invite strategy lies in the developmental theory of the family life cycle. This means that most families experience similar and predictable changes at certain times throughout their maturity. Gathering families or parents of the same stage provides an opportunity for mutual sharing and support. The goal of the focus and invite gathering is to create an atmosphere of safety and trust for folks to realize they are not alone in their family life issues, and that theirs may even be appropriate, healthy struggles for that stage of family life.

The strategy is not intended to fragment parish life into separate groups or cliques. In fact, just the opposite is true. Like-to-like support networks initiated by one's worshiping community provide both personal encouragement to face the challenges of family living and greater motivation to participate in the full life of the parish. These support opportunities also show how the parish can be present to the real life issues that people encounter. Real faith cannot be separated from the clutter and chaos of daily household life.

The Family Life Cycle

Individuals have particular patterns of development. These patterns have been studied carefully by experts such as Erikson on personal development, Kohlberg and Gilligan on moral development, Fowler on faith development, etc. Each of their theories shows predictable stages at which the *individual* must accomplish particular tasks in order to move to the next stage.

The same is true for *families*. There are predictable tasks and issues that all families must deal with at certain stages of their maturity. The developmental stages themselves are not difficult to name. (See Handout V.1) (Note: The family life cycle as described below is "Eriksonian" in nature. In other words it was developed from Erik Erikson's stages of psycho-social development. I used two particular resources in developing the chart itself: 1. *Family Causal Theory: Foundational Frameworks in Family Studies*, Steven Priester, Editor, Catholic University of America, 1980; 2. *Premarital Assessment Skills Training Program*, Rev. Kenneth Metz and John Trokan, Paulist Press, 1987.)

HANDOUT V.1

STAGES OF FAMILY LIFE CYCLE

Family Life Stage	*Developmental Task*	*Characteristic Issues*
1. NEWLY MARRIED	• Intimacy • Commitment to new family system	• Negotiating separateness/belonging • Negotiating roles, friends, money, religion, family planning, sexuality, family of origin, living space
2. NEW PARENT(S)	• Accepting new members • Giving of self to others • Replenishment of self	• Making room for children • Taking on parenting roles • New relationships with extended family re: parenting and grandparenting
3. SCHOOL AGE FAMILY	• Individuation of family members	• Sharing socialization with outside world • Finding a balance between dependence and independence • Household responsibilities • Patterns of communication and conflict resolution

4. ADOLESCENT FAMILY	• Identity vs. identity confusion • Continue with individuation	• Teen shifting in and out of family system • Parents dealing with mid-life marital and career issues • Keeping communication lines open • Working out money matters with teens • Beginning concerns for older generation
5. LAUNCHING FAMILY	• Accepting exits and entries into family • Regrouping as a family	• Refocus on marriage • Children leaving home • Develop adult relationships with children • Meshing with new families—in-laws and grandchildren • Caring for older generation
6. AGING FAMILY	• Integrity vs. despair • Accepting a new generational role	• Retirement • Grandchildren and great-grandchildren • Physical limitations, chronic and/or acute illness • Dependent care • Death of spouse, friends

The oldest child usually determines the stage of development for the family. This is because parents normally expend more energy and anxiety on the issues and concerns that are new to the family. The oldest child carries a special burden because he or she constantly blazes new developmental territory for the entire household. Are any of your team members an oldest child? What was/is it like?

Families must accomplish one or two primary tasks at each stage of development (see Handout V.1). These tasks should not be considered problems, but rather the challenging steps toward family maturity. Problems creep up when families do not deal, or are prevented from dealing, with the tasks at hand. For example, if a young couple does not deal with the issues of "intimacy" before the birth of their first child, they will likely have more difficulty establishing their "couple" living patterns because of all the immediate demands that a new baby brings into the household.

The issues associated with each task (see Handout V.1) give clearer definition to the task itself. For example, "intimacy" is much broader than our normal perception of the term. It encompasses all the factors involved in the process of two persons becoming one family.

These issues also indicate some tension points where families find it difficult to adjust their relationships and boundaries in order to tackle the appropriate task. Transitioning from one stage to the next is always stressful because the relational balance in the family is upset. If one or more family members is changing, the whole family must find a "new" balance. This is seldom easy, but it is necessary for successful movement through the family life cycle.

The more the church, and in particular the parish family ministry team, understands these tasks and points of tension, the better we can assist families with their natural family maturity. We can do a great service for families by simply "greasing" the rough corners of passage. Through peer sharing and like to like ministry, this is just what the strategy of focus and invite seeks to do.

Perhaps you are wondering about single-parent and blended families. Isn't their process of development disrupted? Don't they have unique issues to deal with? Good questions.

As we learned in the first training session, divorce has, to say the least, had a tremendous impact on family life. When separation or divorce occurs, the normal family developmental tasks are often usurped by more basic emotional and physical survival needs. Typical family development is either stalled or thrown into chaos. Parental energies are exhausted, and children are often confused. Some children take on adult responsibilities in a single-parent family, while others act out with disruptive behavior.

Sometimes family members experience a feeling of relief once the separation or divorce actually occurs. After months of strife, there can be peace and calm. Yet the family is forever changed.

As time (and hopefully support) brings healing to the relationships involved, the family can get back on track with their life cycle development. They will likely not be at the same stage they were when it all started and they will certainly see their family issues and tasks through new and learned eyes.

Often, through remarriage, they find themselves in a blended family. The developmental ramifications here are numerous and complex. The household which once was a pre-school family may suddenly be an adolescent family. The oldest child may now be a middle child. Visitations to the non-custodial parent impact patterns of behavior and discipline. Maintaining ties with grandparents may be extremely challenging.

There is no way to "chart" these factors into a tidy, predictable developmental graph. The variables are too numerous. Just remember that all families, regardless of form, must deal with the developmental tasks of each stage of the life cycle. Although they may be postponed for a time, these tasks do not go away.

Even with intact families, it is presumptuous to outline hard and fast categories for their stages of development. Each family is unique, and there is tremendous diversity in family life. Yet the family life cycle is a helpful tool for viewing families in general, understanding their basic concerns, and planning for effective family ministry. This is why we study the family life cycle in preparation for the strategy of focus and invite.

Group Discussion. Take a few minutes to discuss the information presented. Did you learn anything new? Did the information resonate with your family experience? Can you see the value in bringing people of like-needs together?

Implementing Focus and Invite

Overview. Handout V.2 gives a general overview of the steps involved with this strategy.

HANDOUT V.2

FOCUS AND INVITE OVERVIEW

I. *Focus* on a particular developmental stage of family life.

II. *Research* and study the issues, joys and struggles of these families. Tools for researching include books and articles on human development and sociology, surveys, interviews, sharing own experiences, expert consultation, etc.

III. *Resource Gathering.* Pull together available resources that would be helpful in the particular developmental stage.

IV. *Invite* parents or families of the particular stage to come together for one evening.

    A. Prepare list of folks to be invited.

    B. Determine date for gathering.

    C. Write personal invitation. Follow up with phone call.

    D. Use bulletin only as supplementary source of notice.

    E. Ask someone to share his or her experiences and tips from this developmental stage.

V. *Format* for the gathering

    A. Potluck meal (optional)

    B. Welcome and orientation

    C. Structured small group discussion of common issues

    D. Sharing of resources

    E. Exploring options for ongoing enrichment and support

    F. Conclusion

Focus. The first step is choosing the focus group of parents or families. One team member should be delegated to gather census information from the parish office. Using Handout V.3 he or she will try to develop a demographic outline of families in the parish. If census information is computerized, this task should be quite easy. If not, the job may take more time. Yet it is time well spent when you end up with a life cycle portrait of families in your parish. Even if the parish census is not quite up to date, the numbers will reveal helpful information.

HANDOUT V.3

GATHERING CENSUS INFORMATION

How many total households in our parish? _____

How may households in our parish fall under the following categories (according to the age of the oldest child)?

    Beginning family (newly married) _____

    Pre-school family _____

    School age family _____

    Adolescent family _____

    Launching family _____

    Aging family _____

How many two-parent households in our parish? _____

How many single-parent households in our parish? _____

How many households where both parents are employed? _____

How many blended or remarried households? _____

How many interfaith marriage households? _____

The group with the most families should not necessarily be the focus group. Perhaps adequate services are already available to them. Perhaps another group has greater needs. Therefore, in addition to census information, the family ministry team must consider existing services and various needs to determine the focus group.

Research. Once the focus group has been chosen, the family ministry team must learn everything they can about that stage of family life. What are the unique issues, joys and struggles for these families?

Other parish teams have used a variety of ways to research their focus group. Obviously, articles and books, even video programs, are helpful. Some teams have developed simple questionnaires for parents. Others have interviewed folks either by phone or in person. Some teams have consulted local experts for input.

Energetic research into the focus group is important because each team member learns about the focus group, and discovers helpful resources for the focus and invite gathering.

Resource Gathering. In addition to research, the family ministry team must also gather resources for the families of the focus group. These resources should include pertinent articles, books, video programs and a list of available referral services. Your diocesan resource center, parish library and public library are good places to look. The list of referral services is very important because other parish teams have found that usually at least one family shows a need for more specialized, professional help than what the family ministry team can offer.

Your team should gather the actual resources, rather than just compiling a list. Team members should also have some familiarity with these resources.

Invite. You will want to determine the date of your focus and invite gathering as soon as possible. Choose a date and time best suited for those to be invited. You should plan between two and three months ahead from Training Session #3. Take a look at the timeline for this strategy in Handout V.4. This sheet lists all the necessary tasks for hosting your gathering. Begin at the bottom of the sheet by filling in the date of your gathering. Then work your way to the top, filling in appropriate dates. Be sure to make whatever adjustments you deem necessary.

After completing the dates, go back through the list of tasks and assign one or two team members to each task. Some tasks require the full team effort. When your timeline is completed, you have the basic framework for your focus and invite gathering.

HANDOUT V.4

TIMELINE FOR FOCUS AND INVITE

Notation	Date	Person Responsible	Task
Three months prior to gathering		All	Learn about the strategy of focus and invite
Two months prior			Determine date for gathering and reserve room
Two months prior		All	Begin doing research and gathering resources
Six weeks prior			Generate address list of those to be invited
Six weeks prior			Arrange for guest speaker
Six weeks prior			Type up letter of invitation
One month prior			Have letter copied and signed by pastor or team members

One month prior		Address envelopes
Three weeks prior		Send out personal invitations
Two Sundays prior		Bulletin announcement
Two weeks prior	All	Determine exact format and timeline for gathering
Two weeks prior	All	Determine options for ongoing support and enrichment
Seven–nine days prior	All	Follow-up invitation with phone call
One Sunday prior		Bulletin and pulpit announcement
_____	**All**	**Focus and invite gathering**
One–three weeks after		Follow-up as necessary

Invitation Letter. The invitation to your focus group should be done in a personal way. Find out from parish census information and other sources the names, addresses and phone numbers of all those to be invited. Prepare a list and give a copy to each team member.

You may be wondering how to phrase your invitation letter. Naturally, you will want to use your own words, but these sample invitation letters may be a helpful guide (Handouts V.5, V.6). The first letter is written generically, and includes all the components you may wish to use. The other letters were actually used for parish focus and invite gatherings.

HANDOUT V.5

INVITATION LETTER

Date

Dear

 Perhaps you have become aware that our parish now has a family ministry team. We are a group of volunteers who desire to help meet the needs of families in our parish. We are pleased to be of service to you.

 We recognize that yours is a (*name the family life cycle stage*) family. Some issues and concerns that you may be dealing with in your household are:

-

- (highlight some issues common to the stage)

-

-

-

 We invite you to come together on (*date*) with other parents of (*family life cycle stage*) families to talk about these concerns, as well as others. By sharing our struggles and joys with others, we realize that we're not alone and can lend support to one another. The family ministry team has also gathered some resources which you may find interesting and helpful. These will be available for check-out if you wish.

 (*Name of guest[s]*) will take a few minutes to share their joys and struggles as a (*family life cycle stage*) family. Now that they have graduated from this stage, they have wisdom to share with us.

Finally, we will spend time exploring a couple of options for ongoing support and enrichment. This may involve developing a parent support group, or viewing a particular video series, or something of that sort. These ongoing sessions will be completely optional.

The gathering will take place:

(*date*)_____

(*place*)_____

(*time*)_____

One of us from the family ministry team will be calling you soon in order to get an idea of how many folks we can expect. We sincerely hope you can make it. If you have any questions or comments, please call one of us listed below.

Peace in Christ,

St. _____ Family Ministry

(*names & phone #'s*)

HANDOUT V.6

ACTUAL PARISH LETTERS

Dear Friends,

Growing up with and raising teenagers is like nothing else in this world. It has its own set of joys, rewards, and concerns. Only those who either have raised teenagers or are now raising them seem to understand or appreciate these unique joys. In St. Joseph's Parish, families with teenagers make up the largest percentage of our families (almost one-third).

For the past year we, your family ministry team, have been meeting to share hopes, ideas and information about household living. You have seen some of the facts we learned concerning family life in the Sunday bulletin. We are now taking the next step.

We have scheduled a get-together just for those of you raising teenagers. We will be joined by Jim Mahoney, a widely recognized counselor and child and family therapist. His insights and observations when blended with yours will be enlightening and provide hope for all of us.

We hope to see you here:

Rooms 3 & 4
St. Joseph's Parish
Sunday, November 16
7:00 P.M.

The time is designed to coincide with the junior high and senior high youth group meeting times to help with your planning and transportation.

Looking forward to seeing you,

YOUR PARISH FAMILY MINISTRY TEAM

Dear Parents,

We're writing to you because of an event coming up in our parish that focuses on a particular time in parenting that you're living right now. That time is parenting your child from birth through their early years of childhood.

Our guest speaker is committed to the importance of these years of human development and has, in fact, titled them "The Crucial Years," and stated that "this subject of child development, especially from 0-4 years, is the area of deepest interest and passion in my life."

Dr. Kent Hoffman is a psychotherapist at the Marycliff Institute, which is to say, "I am an archaeologist and midwife to the human soul. I believe after fifteen years of doing this work that what I observe on a daily basis is fact—and the fact is that what happens in our earliest years has a radical (root) effect upon all that we experience thereafter."

Kent is father of a three year old child himself, so he is also intimately involved in all the elements that he will speak about.

So, we invite you to come together with other parishioners who are currently parenting children in their early years

on: Tuesday evening, April 26
from: 7:00–8:30 P.M.
at: The Parish Center Annex

Babysitting will be available in the center. Please phone ahead if you plan to use this babysitting service, so we can be sure that your need will be adequately met.

May peace be a product of the tenderness in your home.

SACRED HEART PARISH
FAMILY MINISTRY TEAM

The Gathering. It is very important to plan in detail your focus and invite gathering. In a span of two to three hours, you will want to give participants the opportunity to . . .

- introduce themselves (at least to a few others)
- discuss in small groups common issues and concerns
- view available resources
- hear reflections from a guest speaker
- explore options for ongoing support and enrichment

Handout V.7 gives a detailed description of how you can plan your gathering. Make whatever adjustments you think are necessary. If someone on your team has skills and/or experience with group facilitation, he or she will be a great help with small group discussion and exploring options for ongoing support. In addition to the facilitator, each team member should have a role in the gathering.

HANDOUT V.7

FOCUS AND INVITE GATHERING FORMAT

I. Coffee and Social Time
    (potluck meal is optional)

II. Welcome and Introductions
    • Extend a welcome to all the participants.
    • Family ministry team members introduce themselves.
    • Ask the folks to introduce themselves to those around them.

III. Issues and Concerns for This Stage of Family Life
    • Write on the board four or five issues that are common for the chosen stage of family life.
    • Ask folks to form small groups of six to eight persons. One member from the team should facilitate each group.
    • Say something like this: "On the board we've listed four or five issues and concerns which are common among (*family life cycle stage*) families. We know that these are not the only issues and concerns you have. What other concerns, joys and struggles do you encounter in your family at this time? Take a few minutes to brainstorm in your small group."
    • Have one person in the small groups record the brainstorming on a large piece of newsprint.
    • The recorder shares results with the large group.

IV. Small Group Discussion, Round Two
    • Looking over the list of issues raised, have each person in the small group share "One of the greatest joys about our family life right now is . . ."
    • "One of the greatest struggles about our family life right now is . . ."
    • Have one person from each group share with the large group a summary of their discussion.

BREAK: With opportunity to look at resources.

V. Reflections from Guest Speaker

It is very important for this person not to *give advice* or *tell* the folks how to be better parents. Parents are naturally suspicious and defensive in such situations. This person should share some struggles and joys that his or her family experienced while in that stage, and how the family has grown from their experience.

VI. Options for Ongoing Support and Enrichment

Some general guidelines for options:
- make at least two options available to the large group
- each option must be simple and easy to implement
- each option should involve no more than six sessions
- the leader or facilitator of a small group should *not* be a family ministry team member
- a team member should be prepared to train the facilitator
- all necessary materials should be on hand for inspection by those who are interested
- the options should vary in format, times and focus
- Briefly summarize each option for the large group. Remind people that these activities are purely optional. They do not have to participate if they do not wish.
- Break into small groups according to interest. A team member should lead each small group, giving further explanation of the option. The team member should also help establish times and place for the sessions, but should be clear that he or she is not the primary leader.

VIII. Conclusion
- Summarize decisions from small groups
- Closing prayer

Options for Ongoing Support and Enrichment. This is a crucial component of the focus and invite gathering. Remember, not everyone will want to participate. Some will feel they are too busy to commit themselves to a support group, even for a short while. Some will not be interested in follow-up. They may, however, take an article or something home to read and share with others. The point: the options are completely optional.

For those who wish to take part in an ongoing option, they may need some initial assistance. One team member should be available to provide this assistance. However, he or she should pull back and leave the group to their own leadership once they are up and rolling.

You are probably wondering how to provide for ongoing options and where to get the materials. First, some general guidelines:

- Choose materials that are easy to use.
- Choose options that are short term. Initially, groups should be asked to come together no more than four to six times. This provides an automatic break for some folks to drop off if that is their desire. If the group wishes to continue after the initial sessions, that is terrific, and more material can be found for them.
- One of your family ministry team members may be needed to help get the group started. However, he or she should not become the leader or facilitator of the group. Why? Because once the group is launched, the team member should drop away and let them be autonomous.

Perhaps the best materials for ongoing options are video programs (with study guides) that pertain to the chosen stage of family life. These may address such issues as parenting, family communication, family faith development, marriage enrichment, etc. Video programs are appealing because they can be borrowed from the parish or diocesan office and used in the home.

Several parish teams have also used written materials such as workbooks for developing parenting skills or scripture study, etc. The key to any of these materials is simplicity and ease of use. The group facilitator should not have to be an expert educator to use the materials.

Several other groups have not used any materials at all. They simply arrange to meet together for several sessions to talk informally about their family situations. Often, just dessert and a cup of coffee provide plenty of "food" for discussion among folks who encounter similar experiences.

Because of the vastness of the family life cycle stages, it is not possible here to mention all the available materials. After you've determined your focus, you should be able to find appropriate materials in your parish resource library or religious education office. Ask your parish religious education coordinator. You should also consult with your diocesan resource center, family life office and religious education office. Don't hesitate to call these offices, even if you have never done so before. They are there to serve all folks involved in parish ministry. You may also find helpful materials in your public library.

Parish Variations to Focus and Invite. It is not possible to describe how each parish team has implemented this strategy. However, every team with whom I have worked has done it differently. There is much room for creativity and variation. Below are some of these variations that teams have employed.

- Several teams have sponsored a pot-luck supper in connection with their gathering.
- Several teams have sponsored their gathering on the same night as religious education classes or youth group. Some have even concluded the evening by bringing the two groups together.
- Several teams have provided child care during their gatherings, particularly if the focus group was pre-school, school-age or single-parent families.
- One team had their gathering on Sunday morning between masses.
- One team deliberately planned two consecutive sessions, each a week apart. They simply wanted to have more time to address each component of the gathering.
- One team invited everyone, including the guest speaker, back six months later for a large group follow-up session.
- One team sponsored their gathering in late spring and focused on "Creative Summer Family Fun and Faith Activities."

Hopefully, these variations will initiate some creativity of your own.

Implications for Family Spirituality

Throughout the stages of the family life cycle, families grow and share their faith in different ways. Just as their social, educational and support needs are different at each stage, so too are their household spiritual needs. When folks of similar needs gather together, they can explore avenues of faith growth and spirituality in an atmosphere of mutual trust and support. Clustering families together can sometimes lead a family to engage in spiritual and prayerful expressions that they might not otherwise have had the courage to try by themselves at home.

Passage from one stage to another also provides an excellent time for families to discover the gracious activity of God in their lives. Often there is a brief window of spiritual openness amid the struggle and confusion of family change. Hopefully the focus and invite gathering can help folks recognize this openness and respond to it.

Throughout history, God has been present to those experiencing transition and change. Change is never easy, and families naturally resist it. Sometimes God gives them courage to embrace it and adjust their lives to it. At other times, God is discovered in the midst of the struggle.

Periods of transition and life passage also offer a momentary chance for healing in the family. If perhaps the family has been living with an unreconciled hurt, an opportunity for healing sometimes emerges as they adjust to a different stage of family life.

For all these reasons, the strategy of focus and invite provides excellent opportunities to enhance family spirituality.

Team Planning Time

Now that your team has been fully oriented to this strategy, take the remainder of your time to begin planning for your gathering. Use the focus and invite timeline (Handout V.4) as your guide, and be sure to answer, "*Who* will do *what* by *when*?"

Conclusion

Your team will likely have to meet a few times as you implement this strategy. It would be smart to schedule those meetings now.

Remind team members that Training Session #4 will happen sometime shortly after your successful focus and invite gathering. Of course it will be successful!

Closing Prayer. Recall the prayer theme and readings for this session. Theme: "Building a Strong Family Foundation." Readings: Matthew 7:24-27 and Ephesians 2:20-22.

VI

Training Session #4

Assessment of Team Progress and Developing Leadership in Parish Family Ministry

Partnership between parish and families is possible. A parish with a high Hispanic population developed an alternative catechetical program for first eucharist. Actually, it was the Hispanic parents who were preparing their children in family clusters. They used a published program from Mexico that was more sensitive to their native language and culture. They then announced to the pastor that their children were ready to receive first communion. The partnership was established when the pastor agreed that the children were indeed ready for first communion even though they had not participated in the "official" parish program.

The focus of this session is assessing the progress of the family ministry team with the three strategies: awareness raising, family sensitivity in parish ministry, and focus and invite. Your team will also explore some important principles for effective partnership between parish life and family life. Several common obstacles to this partnership will also be noted. After discussing implications for family spirituality, your team will conclude this session by establishing plans for the future with respect to the three strategies. As mentioned, this session should happen after the team has completed their first focus and invite gathering.

For the Project Coordinator

If you are tempted to skip this training session because it may not seem important enough, I implore you not to do so. Even though no new strategy is introduced, this training session is essential. Assessment of progress is extremely valuable for *ongoing,* effective parish family ministry. Too often we get caught up in our immediate tasks and fail to step back and look at the whole picture. Doing so can help realign the overall direction of your work.

The presentation you will give is "Family Life in Partnership with Parish Life." Exploring the principles of and obstacles to partnership is key for effective ministry of any kind, including family ministry. All services in the parish are connected. All ministries impact the family. Without partnership and collaboration, there is no possibility for effective ministry and service in the parish.

The prayer theme and scripture readings are listed below.

One more important point. Your objective for this session is to ensure that the team determines its goals and steps for the future. They must now set their own agenda and, in light of the three strategies, decide where to focus their energies. By the end of this session, the team should know just what it will be doing in future months.

Training Session Outline

I.   Welcome, Orientation and Prayer (allow 10 minutes)

II. Project Evaluation (allow 45 minutes)
    A. Team members complete evaluation form
    B. Group discussion

III. Where Do We Go from Here? (allow 25 minutes)
    A. Renewing my commitment to the team
    B. Recruiting new team members

IV. Family Life in Partnership with Parish Life (allow 45 minutes)
    A. Principles of partnership
    B. Common obstacles to partnership
    C. Group discussion

V.   Conclusion (allow 25 minutes)
    A. Review plans for the future
    B. Closing prayer

Welcome, Orientation and Prayer

The project coordinator gives a brief introduction to this last training session. Use the information and outline above. Stress the importance of evaluation and assessment. Hopefully your team has developed a positive trust level by now so that each member can be honest and straightforward with their comments. This is particularly important when talking about whether or not to continue serving on the family ministry team.

Opening Prayer. The theme for this session is "Contributing Our Gifts to the One Body Of Christ." The scripture readings are 1 Corinthians 12:4-7 and 1 Corinthians 12:12-20.

Project Evaluation

Before team members fill out the evaluation form, the project coordinator should review the strategies of the *Caring That Enables* project:

- Family Life Awareness Raising—using the tools of communication in the parish to raise consciousness of the realities of marriage and family life today.
- Family Sensitivity in Parish Ministry—partnering with other ministries to bring a "family perspective" to those ministries and services.
- Focus and Invite—focusing on a group of parents or families of like needs, and inviting them together for mutual support and enrichment.

With this as an introduction, the team members are ready to complete the evaluation form (Handout VI.1). They will need approximately fifteen minutes.

HANDOUT VI.1

PROJECT EVALUATION

The *Caring That Enables* project attempts to communicate three key strategies for parish family ministry:
- Family Life Awareness Raising
- Family Sensitivity in Parish Ministry
- Focus and Invite

Part I: Evaluation of the Project Itself

1. How well were the three strategies communicated in the training sessions?

- Family Life Awareness Raising

poor	fair	excellent		
1	2	3	4	5

- Family Sensitivity in Parish Ministry

1	2	3	4	5

- Focus and Invite

1	2	3	4	5

Comments:

2. What has been most valuable for you in the *Caring That Enables* project?

3. What has been least valuable?

4. What would you change about the *Caring That Enables* project?

Part II: Evaluation of Your Team Performance

5. Has your team implemented the three strategies?

- Family Life Awareness Raising   ___yes ___no
  level of success: 1   2   3   4   5

- Family Sensitivity in Parish Ministry   ___yes ___no
  level of success: 1   2   3   4   5

- Focus and Invite   ___yes ___no
  level of success: 1   2   3   4   5

Comments:

6. If a new person joined your parish family ministry team, would you be able to effectively communicate the three strategies to that person?

    1   2   3   4   5

Comments:

7. Is there evidence that your team has contributed to the health of families in your parish?

8. What specific direction/project should your team take on for next year?

9. Do you intend to continue serving on the parish family ministry team?

10. Will your team need new volunteers for next year?

Discussion. For the next thirty minutes or so, discuss each of the questions in Part II of the evaluation. Someone on the team should take notes so that whatever ideas and plans for the future are mentioned will be recorded. This discussion often reveals several areas of need and project ideas for the family ministry team to pursue. It it seems beneficial now, go ahead and put some flesh to whatever new ideas and plans are generated. You will come back to these at the end of this training session.

Where Do We Go from Here?

Renewing My Commitment to the Team. Teams are encouraged to discuss the last two questions of the evaluation in a candid, yet sensitive manner. Members should not be pressured to continue their commitment if they do not wish. If a member decides not to commit for another year, perhaps he or she can suggest a couple of others as replacement.

Recruiting New Team Members. In most parishes, finding volunteers for any service takes some recruiting. Seldom do they just walk up and announce they would like to help—although, if you've been effective in implementing the three strategies, it would not be so unusual for someone to do just that.

Presuming, though, that you will have to do some recruiting, here are a few tips (Handout VI.2). Read these tips aloud with the team, and offer whatever comments and examples might be appropriate. Be sure to allow others to comment also. Refer to Chapter II, "Selecting the Volunteer Team," for a fuller description of these tips.

HANDOUT VI.2

TIPS FOR RECRUITING TEAM MEMBERS

- Look for "natural leaders."

- Look for "successful transitioners"—people who have grown through stresses of family transition such as new-lywed to developing family, or newly divorced to single-parent lifestyle.

- Look for folks to fill out the diversity of your team.

- Use a personal approach to recruit new members. One-to-one contact always works best.

- Be specific about what you are asking them to do. How much time is involved? How many meetings? How much extra work? How long is the commitment? etc. Provide a job description.

- Name the person's gifts and talents. Assure him or her that you believe he or she can do the job. Many people do not volunteer because they feel they are inadequate. A little flattery can go a long way.

- Always give the person a chance to say "no." People who say "yes" reluctantly make lousy volunteers.

- Provide necessary orientation and training for new members.

- Provide all necessary materials, handouts and resources for new members.

After reviewing these tips, the team should then brainstorm names of individuals who might serve well on the family ministry team. After compiling a list, however short or long, decide how to contact these people in a personal and affirmative way. Remember, always give permission to say "no." Family ministry should be the last place where we arm-twist people to volunteer.

Even if your team does not need new volunteers now, these tips should be read and discussed. It is helpful information to have when the need arises.

After you have discussed the evaluation questions to the satisfaction of everyone, collect the form from each team member. Perhaps you will want to give a summary of these evaluations to your pastor, parish staff or parish council. If your team has begun generating ideas for next year, ask them to hold off on their planning while you give your presentation on "partnership."

Family Life in Partnership with Parish Life

This segment of the training session focuses on collaboration and partnership in ministry. The goal is for team members to realize that all parish ministries are interconnected, and therefore effective family ministry must work in partnership with all other services in the parish.

In a manner that suits you best, communicate the information below to your family ministry team.

The strategies of family ministry we have tried to employ require us to be like Jesus: the son of a carpenter standing on the shore telling fishermen how to fish (John 21). It's a bit of a paradox, but it tells us that we must approach folks in other ministries with diplomacy and even a little flattery. This is the beginning of effective partnership.

Family ministry should never be done in isolation from, or in competition with, other ministries and services in the parish. Even if we enjoy success and gain prominence over the others, the ones who lose in the end are families themselves. This is why we do not advocate for more "programs," even family life programs. Too often it creates competition rather than collaboration.

Principles of Effective Partnership. What does effective partnership look like? What are some important ingredients for a healthy relationship between family life and parish life? Handout VI.3 highlights several principles. Read these and discuss their importance and relevance.

HANDOUT VI.3

PRINCIPLES OF PARTNERSHIP

1. There must be an atmosphere of mutual respect. We recognize your strengths, gifts and talents, and your needs.

2. Each party must be self-defined. We know what our values are. We know our goals and our hopes for the future.

3. Each party must understand and recognize the need for interdependence. We are not totally dependent on you, nor completely independent from you.

4. Each party has desirable/necessary qualities. We are happy to contribute our gifts and talents for the good of others.

5. Each party can contribute only from a stance of health and strength. When we feel inferior and put down, we cannot recognize our gifts to share. Focus on strengths rather than dysfunction.

6. There must be an open channel of communication. We cannot be partners unless we listen to and communicate openly with each other.

7. Changing old patterns is not easy. We understand the nature of resistance to change.

When we treat others as equals, with gifts to share and a piece of the "truth" to impart, they will be much more willing to engage in partnership and treat us the same way.

Obstacles to Effective Partnership. The principles listed above are obvious and logical. So why don't we have more and better partnerships in the world and in the church? Genuine partnership implies change and compromise, and people usually resist change. Noted theologian David M. Thomas highlights eight common obstacles to effective partnership. Many times we are guilty of one or another of these attitudes without being aware of it.

1. *Competitiveness.* "I must win in order to build my self-esteem. In order to win, I must put others down."

2. *Small-Mindedness.* "My world is the only world. The boundaries of the world cannot reach beyond my desk."

3. *Arrogance.* "I am better than the rest. My ideas are better, and my way of doing things is certainly better. So why should I partner with you?"

4. *Inferiority.* "I can't offer anything. I am not nearly as smart or creative as the others."

5. *Perfectionism.* "I will not do it unless we do it perfectly. I cannot stand to lose control over the project."

6. *Burnout.* "Let's not try anything new. I have *so* much to do as it is." Cynicism often accompanies burnout.

7. *No Experience of Success.* "It'll never work. We tried that once, and it didn't fly."

8. *Fear of Conflict.* "Let's not make waves."

Chances are everyone carries around one or two of these attitudes. Yet if we acknowledge them, it is possible to dispel their mythical, illogical nature. We must do so in ourselves first, before approaching others.

The Program Continuum. Another way of looking at partnership is through the "program continuum." In his book *A New Design for Family Ministry*, Dennis Guernsey describes four types of partnership between families and congregation—two that are negative and two that are positive.

On the negative end of the continuum is the "parasitic approach" to ministry. This model demands unfailing commitment to all activities. The virtue of service gets turned around. Families find themselves sustaining parish programs instead of being served by them. It will even go so far as to equate one's level of activity to one's commitment to Christ.

The "competitive approach" is less severe, yet more common in parish programs. With the calendar as a battlefield, we often skirmish over the best nights for our activities. Working around school and community events, we schedule activities during the remaining prime time. Families lose out. They have only "leftover" time to spend together. Family members become resistant because it seems the program is constantly demanding more and more. Motivation begins to wane, and resentments build. Parish ministers find themselves constantly seeking new volunteers to replace those who have been expended in battle.

Moving to the positive side of the continuum, the best image for the "cooperative approach" to parish programming is *friendship*. This model seeks creative ways to work within the rhythms of family life and to protect family relationships. The best thing about friendship: people are free to say "no." A cooperative model knows that as its families flourish, so will the parish.

On the far positive end of the continuum is the "symbiotic approach." This model typifies a mutually interdependent relationship between the parish program and families. The health or illness of one is clearly experienced by the other. This "symbiosis" seldom occurs in a large parish, but is not uncommon among small groups and clusters in the faith community.

More is not always better. Careful planning which recognizes the limitations of a family's time, space and energy will yield balanced and dynamic parish programs. And folks might enjoy a night at home!

Portraits of Success. Partnership is possible—one small step at a time. I worked with one parish that collaborated with several other churches in their small town. They approached their public school board about declaring one night a week free from all school activities. This included games, practices, concerts—everything. After succeeding with the school board, the parish then split the free evenings with families. One night was church night, and the next week it was family night. They also provided creative suggestions for how families might spend their time together at home.

Another parish brought together people from a variety of ministries to address the issue of human sexuality from a holistic, family-based approach. The sensitive nature of the topic motivated ministers and families to work together. Nobody wanted to tackle this one by themselves, yet creating an accepting, sensitive atmosphere of collaboration was the challenging key to this partnership.

Partnership, like families themselves, is seldom neat and tidy. Rather, it is messy and even chaotic at times. We have to give up our need to control, and yet remain true to our responsibility to participate in the process. Each partner holds a piece of the "truth."

Implications for Family Spirituality

What does partnership have to do with family faith growth? Families need their parishes to grow in faith. They cannot go it alone. Families must be challenged to enter the communal faith life in order to be enriched by others. As the community listens, supports, nourishes and guides families in their household struggles and joys, so too the parish can evangelize and catechize the family.

But it must be a mutual relationship. Parishes need families also. Christian families are the foundational church. Parishes cannot go it alone. Parish communities are challenged to recognize the day-to-day issues of household living, and make the gospel message meaningful in that arena. Jesus talked "fishing" with fishermen and "farming" with farmers. True partnership will impact the life experience of both families and parishes.

Discussion. Take a few minutes to discuss the importance and implications of partnership. Did you learn anything new? How should your parish family ministry team respond to the challenge of partnership?

Conclusion

In light of the presentation and discussion on partnership, review the ideas and plans your team generated earlier in the session.

- Are there any new ideas for how your team should proceed?
- Which ideas will the team take on? Do the ideas need to be changed or adjusted?
- *Who* will do *what* by *when?*
- Schedule a date, time, and place for your next meeting.

Closing Prayer. Recall the prayer theme and readings for this session. Theme: "Contributing Our Gifts to the One Body of Christ." Readings: 1 Corinthians 12:4-7 and 1 Corinthians 12:12-20.